PATRICK H. PERRINE

Daring Disruption

An Entrepreneur's Guide to Igniting Innovation and Creativity for Extraordinary Business Success

"Each person deserves a day away in which no problems are confronted, no solutions searched for. Each of us needs to withdraw from the cares which will not withdraw from us."

— Maya Angelou

Contents

Preface

In the dynamic arena of today's business world, where change is the only constant, 'Daring Disruption: An Entrepreneur's Guide to Igniting Innovation and Creativity for Extraordinary Business Success' emerges as your beacon through the fog of competition and rapid evolution. This fifth volume in the 'Be A Unicorn' series directly builds upon the foundation laid in Step 5 of 'Unicorn Rising,' taking a deep dive into the realms of innovation and creativity that are pivotal for any entrepreneurial venture aiming to leave an indelible mark on the industry.

As the latest installment in a series designed to guide entrepreneurs from ideation to acquisition, 'Daring Disruption' is more than a book; it's a comprehensive workbook that interweaves the threads of innovative thinking and creative problem-solving with actionable strategies, exercises, and real-world case studies. This approach ensures that the insights you gather here are not just conceptual but are immediately applicable to your entrepreneurial journey.

Innovation, as we explore in these pages, is not confined to the echelons of technology giants or the sudden spark of a groundbreaking invention. It encompasses a broad spectrum of activities and mindsets, from making incremental improvements to achieving disruptive breakthroughs. Creativity, the counterpart of innovation, is the wellspring of this transformative power, enabling you to see beyond the conventional and harness the potential of what could be.

This book invites you to embark on a journey of discovery, where the synergy of innovation and creativity becomes your most powerful tool in navigating the entrepreneurial landscape. Through a carefully curated exploration of innovative methodologies, leadership insights for fostering a creative culture, and inspirations drawn from industry disruptors, 'Daring Disruption' aims to equip you with the skills to think differently, act boldly, and realize the extraordinary potential of your business ideas.

Join us as we traverse the multifaceted dimensions of innovation and creativity, aimed at empowering you, the entrepreneur, to not only dream of disruptive ideas but to bring them to fruition with confidence and strategic finesse. 'Daring Disruption' is your guide to transforming challenges into opportunities for growth, leveraging the untapped potential within your venture, and sculpting a future where your business not only succeeds but thrives on the cutting edge of innovation.

Welcome to the journey of 'Daring Disruption.' Here, we unlock the secrets to not just surviving but flourishing in the ever-evolving business ecosystem, armed with innovation, creativity, and the unwavering spirit of entrepreneurship. Let's ignite the spark of disruptive thinking and turn the wheels of extraordinary business success together.

Be A Unicorn: The New Entrepreneur's Ultimate Guide To Success

Dream It, Build It:
An Aspirational Odyssey Through
Entrepreneurship in Ten Inspiring Volumes.

Volume Five

DARING DISRUPTION
An Entrepreneur's Guide to Igniting Innovation and
Creativity for Extraordinary Business Success

1

Understanding Innovation: The Bedrock of Extraordinary Success

"Innovation is not about saying yes to everything.
It's about saying no to all but the most crucial
features."
— Steve Jobs

Stepping into the arena of disruption, "Daring Disruption" invites entrepreneurs to master the art of innovation, the cornerstone of unprecedented success. In a world where change is the only constant, innovation becomes the compass that guides businesses through uncharted territories, turning obstacles into stepping stones for growth. This chapter unravels the complexities of innovation, illuminating its pivotal role in sculpting businesses that not only thrive but also leave a lasting imprint on their industries. It is a narrative that champions the transformative power of saying "no," allowing entrepreneurs to focus on what truly matters and to sculpt ventures of significance from the ground up.

This journey through innovation is not a solitary endeavor but a collaborative voyage, inviting thinkers, makers, and doers to converge on a platform where creativity meets execution. Here, innovation is demystified, presented not merely as a buzzword but as a tangible process of continuous evolution, driving businesses forward in their quest for excellence. Through the lens of innovation, we explore the myriad ways in which businesses can navigate the ever-evolving landscape of consumer needs, technological advancements, and competitive dynamics.

At the heart of "Daring Disruption" lies the conviction that innovation is the lifeblood of extraordinary success. It challenges entrepreneurs to transcend traditional boundaries, to reimagine the fabric of their industries, and to forge new paradigms of value creation. This chapter is a clarion call to action, urging business leaders to cultivate a mindset of relentless innovation, to harness the collective genius of their teams, and to embark on a journey of creating the future, one disruptive idea at a time.

Opening Anecdote: Navigating Choppy Waters: the Story of Kickstarter's Launch

Kickstarter, founded by Perry Chen, Yancey Strickler, and Charles Adler, faced a major obstacle in 2012 when they experienced a security breach that compromised their users' data. Faced with potential backlash and loss of trust, the trio responded swiftly, communicating transparently with their community and implementing enhanced security measures. Their proactive approach not only restored confidence in the platform but also demonstrated their commitment to safe-guarding user interests, laying the foundation for Kickstarter's continued success.

Why This Guide? This volume is more than just a continuation of a conversation on entrepreneurship; it's a deep dive into the heart of innovation and creativity. It's designed to equip you with the knowledge, strategies, and inspiration to transform challenges into opportunities for groundbreaking success. Through a mix of theoretical insights, practical advice, and real-world examples, we aim to guide you through the intricacies of fostering an environment where innovation thrives.

The Pillars of Innovation: Innovation is a multifaceted phenomenon that extends beyond mere invention. It encompasses a wide array of practices—from product and process innovation to business model and organizational innovation. Each type serves as a critical component in the tapestry of business growth and competitiveness, shaping the way companies create value and sustain their market position.

The Innovation Ecosystem: A vibrant innovation ecosystem is pivotal for nurturing groundbreaking ideas. This ecosystem is composed of various stakeholders, including customers, employees, partners, and the broader community. Each plays a crucial role in supporting the innovation process, offering unique perspectives and resources that can spur creativity and drive progress.

Defining Innovation: At its core, innovation is the process of implementing new ideas, processes, or products to create significant value. It's about seeing beyond the present, anticipating future needs, and bringing to life solutions that meet those needs in novel and effective ways. We'll explore the dimensions of innovation, from incremental improvements that enhance existing offerings to disruptive breakthroughs that redefine industries.

Exploring the Role of Innovation in Business: Innovation is the engine of competitive advantage and business growth. It enables organizations to differentiate themselves, capture new markets, and respond dynamically to changing customer demands and technological advances. We will dissect how innovation can be systematically fostered within your organization to ensure sustained success.

Types of Innovation: Understanding the different types of innovation is crucial for recognizing the breadth of opportunities available. Whether it's revolutionizing your product line, streamlining your operations, reimagining your business model, or cultivating a culture that champions creative thinking, each form of innovation holds the potential to drive significant business impact.

Conclusion: As we embark on this exploration of innovation, remember that it's not just about generating ideas; it's about executing those ideas effectively to achieve real impact. The journey ahead is designed to unlock the transformative power of innovation and creativity, laying the groundwork for you to lead your business toward extraordinary success.

Ready to dive deeper into the mechanisms of innovation and creativity? Let's move forward, armed with the insights and strategies necessary to navigate the complexities of today's business world and emerge as a true disruptor.

2

The Innovation Mindset: Nurturing the Seeds of Disruption

"Mindset is everything. What you think, you become."
— Buddha

Embarking on the transformative journey detailed in "Daring Disruption," this chapter delves deep into the crux of entrepreneurial excellence: the innovation mindset. It's not merely about adopting new ideas or technologies; it's about fostering a culture that champions creativity, curiosity, and the courage to defy conventional norms. Here, we uncover the essential elements of an innovation mindset—curiosity, openness to change, risk-taking, adaptability, and a growth mindset—underscored by collaboration and diversity. These foundational pillars are exemplified by industry leaders like Google's encouragement of curiosity through personal projects, IBM's reinvention through openness to change, Amazon's culture of risk-taking, Netflix's adaptability in business models, and Microsoft's dedication to fostering a growth mindset.

The innovation mindset is the fertile ground from which groundbreaking ideas sprout, thrive, and disrupt industries. By examining real-world applications from companies like Google, IBM, and Amazon, to transformative strategies that encourage experimentation and learning, this chapter is both a blueprint and a beacon for those ready to navigate the tumultuous yet rewarding seas of innovation.

Opening Anecdote: A Spark of Brilliance: The Origin Story of Spanx

Sara Blakely, the founder of Spanx, experienced numerous setbacks on her journey to success. From facing rejection by potential investors to grappling with manufacturing challenges, Blakely's resilience and innovative spirit were put to the test. However, her unwavering belief in her product and her willingness to think outside the box eventually paid off. Today, Spanx is a household name, revolutionizing the fashion industry with its innovative shapewear solutions.

Quick Thought:
True innovation begins in the mind. It's a product of how we see the world and our belief in the possibility of change.

Entrepreneurship in Action: Key Ingredients

- **Curiosity and Questioning:** At the heart of innovation

lies an insatiable curiosity and the courage to question norms.

- **Risk-taking and Resilience:** Embracing failure as a stepping stone, not a setback, fosters a culture of bold experimentation.
- **Collaboration and Diversity:** Diverse teams bring together varied perspectives, igniting creativity and unveiling novel solutions.

Case Study: Tesla's Electric Revolution

Elon Musk's vision and Tesla's overcoming of skepticism through continuous innovation underscore the importance of adaptability and risk-taking in pioneering sustainable automotive solutions.

- **The Vision:** Elon Musk's ambition to accelerate the world's transition to sustainable energy.
- **The Challenge:** Overcoming skepticism and technological barriers to electric vehicles.
- **The Strategy:** Continuous innovation, from battery technology to self-driving capabilities.
- **The Impact:** Tesla has not only become a leader in electric vehicles but has also shifted global automotive industry standards towards sustainability.

Case Study: Airbnb's Disruptive Platform

Airbnb's transformation of the travel accommodation industry highlights the power of innovative thinking and openness to change, focusing on user experience and community building.

- **The Idea:** Transforming the concept of accommodation by connecting travelers with local hosts.
- **The Obstacle:** Building trust and scaling a platform-based business in a traditional industry.
- **The Approach:** Focusing on user experience, community building, and innovative technology.
- **The Outcome:** Airbnb revolutionized the travel industry, making personalized and affordable accommodations accessible worldwide.

Pro Tip: Foster an environment where every challenge is viewed as a gateway to innovation. Encourage your team to see obstacles as opportunities to learn and grow.

Strategies for Cultivating an Innovation Mindset

1. **Encourage Experimentation:** Embrace a culture of trial and error, akin to 3M's "15% time" policy, where failure is seen as a growth opportunity.
2. **Foster a Learning Culture:** Like Microsoft's growth mindset initiative, promote ongoing learning and development, pushing for continuous innovation.
3. **Promote Cross-Functional Collaboration:** Encourage collaboration across diverse teams, leveraging varied perspectives for richer, more inventive solutions.
4. **Recognize and Reward Innovation:** Celebrate innovative efforts, reinforcing the value placed on creative and new ideas, motivating ongoing innovation.

Exercise: Cultivating an Innovation Mindset

Reflecting on Failures and Lessons Learned:

1. Reflect on a recent challenge or failure you've encountered, either professionally or personally. Take time to analyze the circumstances surrounding it and identify the key lessons you learned from the experience.
2. Consider how these lessons can serve as valuable insights for future innovation endeavors. Explore ways in which you can leverage these insights to approach future challenges with resilience and creativity.

Exploring New Horizons and Stimulating Creativity:

1. Challenge yourself to spend a week immersing in topics or activities outside your usual scope of interest or expertise. Engage in activities such as reading diverse articles, attending workshops or lectures, or exploring hobbies unrelated to your field.
2. Take note of any fresh perspectives, ideas, or connections that emerge as a result of this exploration. Reflect on how exposing yourself to new experiences and knowledge can ignite creativity and inspire innovative thinking.

Facilitating Collaborative Brainstorming Sessions:

1. Organize a collaborative brainstorming session with colleagues from various departments or areas of expertise within your organization. Create a conducive environment for open dialogue and idea-sharing.

2. Observe how the diverse perspectives and backgrounds of participants contribute to the generation of innovative solutions. Encourage active participation and cross-pollination of ideas to foster creativity and drive collective problem-solving efforts.

Challenge For You:
Pinpoint a stagnant area in your life or work. Employ the innovation mindset to conceptualize a unique solution. Reflect on how your distinct skills and perspectives can drive innovation.

Conclusion:
Embracing the innovation mindset is vital for anyone aspiring to make a significant impact in the entrepreneurial landscape. It's about envisioning the unseen, believing in the improbable, and achieving the extraordinary. This chapter, enriched with detailed explorations, real-world examples, and actionable strategies, equips you to navigate the complexities of innovation with confidence. As we progress, let this mindset guide you through the realms of creativity and disruption, transforming challenges into opportunities for groundbreaking success.

3

Design Thinking: A Human-Centered Approach to Innovation

"I want every little girl who's told she's bossy to be told instead that she has leadership skills."
— Sheryl Sandberg

D elving into the essence of entrepreneurial excellence, this chapter explores the innovation mindset, highlighting it as not just about adopting new ideas or technologies but about fostering a culture that champions creativity, curiosity, and the courage to defy conventional norms. We uncover the essential elements of an innovation mindset—curiosity, openness to change, risk-taking, adaptability, and a growth mindset—underscored by collaboration and diversity. These foundational pillars, exemplified by industry leaders like Google's encouragement of curiosity through personal projects, IBM's reinvention through openness to change, Amazon's culture of risk-taking, Netflix's adaptability in business models, and Microsoft's dedication to fostering a growth mindset, provide the fertile ground from which groundbreaking ideas sprout, thrive, and disrupt industries. By examining real-world applications from companies like Google, IBM, and Amazon, to transformative strategies that encourage experimentation and learning, we present both a blueprint and a beacon for those prepared to navigate the tumultuous yet rewarding seas of innovation.

Opening Anecdote: Airbnb's Humble Beginnings: From Air Mattresses to Hospitality Giant

In 2008, Brian Chesky and Joe Gebbia, the co-founders of Airbnb, faced a daunting challenge when they struggled to pay their rent in San Francisco. To generate extra income, they decided to rent out air mattresses in their living room to attendees of a local conference. This unconventional idea laid the foundation for what would become a global hospitality phenomenon. By focusing on the needs and experiences of their users, Chesky and Gebbia transformed the travel industry and disrupted the traditional hotel model.

Quick Thought:
Empathy isn't just about understanding others; it's about letting that understanding guide our innovations.

Entrepreneurship in Action: Key Ingredients

- **Empathy:** Begin with genuine curiosity about the people you're designing for. Deeply understanding their lives, challenges, and needs is the cornerstone of impactful

solutions.
- **Collaborative Ideation:** Leverage diverse perspectives. Bringing together different minds leads to more creative, comprehensive solutions.
- **Iterative Prototyping:** Embrace the process of creating, testing, learning, and iterating. Each cycle brings you closer to a solution that resonates with your users.

Case Study: IDEO's Shopping Cart Project

Background: IDEO, a renowned design and consulting firm, took on the challenge of redesigning the everyday shopping cart to enhance the overall shopping experience. The traditional shopping cart, while functional, often presented usability issues and failed to consider the diverse needs of shoppers. IDEO aimed to revolutionize this mundane object, leveraging design thinking principles to create a more user-centric solution.

Approach: IDEO's multidisciplinary team immersed themselves in the shopping experience, observing shoppers in various environments, from grocery stores to hardware stores. They engaged in empathetic conversations with shoppers and store employees to understand pain points and opportunities for improvement. By conducting in-depth interviews and hands-on research, IDEO gained valuable insights into the complexities of the shopping journey.

Solution: Drawing from their research and ideation sessions, IDEO prototyped a new shopping cart design that addressed key usability issues and incorporated innovative features to enhance the overall shopping experience. The new cart was designed to be more maneuverable, modular to accommodate different shopping needs, and equipped with a built-in scanner for instant checkout. Additionally, IDEO explored sustainable materials and manufacturing processes to minimize environmental impact.

Impact: While the redesigned shopping cart was initially a prototype, it sparked conversations and inspired further innovation in the retail industry. IDEO's emphasis on user-centric design and functionality set a new standard for shopping cart design, prompting retailers to rethink their approach to the shopping experience. Although the redesigned cart may not have been widely adopted, its impact on the industry's perception of user-centered design was profound.

Legacy and Insights: IDEO's Shopping Cart Project serves as a compelling example of the power of design thinking in reimagining everyday objects. By prioritizing empathy, collaboration, and iterative prototyping, IDEO was able to create a solution that not only addressed usability issues but also sparked innovation in the retail industry. This case study highlights the transformative potential of human-centered design in solving complex challenges and shaping the future of product design and innovation.

```
Pro Tip: Always circle back to your users. Their
feedback is invaluable in refining your solution to
ensure it truly meets their needs and exceeds their
expectations.
```

Exercise: Empathy-Driven Innovation Exploration

Empathy Mapping for Insightful Problem-Solving:

1. Select a problem or challenge that resonates with you and holds personal significance. Dedicate a day to immerse yourself in the environment or community affected by this issue.
2. Engage in active observation and conversation with individuals impacted by the problem. Take note of their thoughts, feelings, behaviors, and pain points related to the issue.
3. Create an empathy map to visually represent your findings, including key insights, emotions, needs, and aspirations of the individuals you interacted with. Use this empathetic understanding as a foundation for designing meaningful solutions.

Creative Idea Generation for Innovative Solutions:

1. Utilizing the insights gathered from your empathy mapping exercise, embark on a brainstorming session to generate potential solutions to the identified problem. Encourage the exploration of diverse ideas, no matter how unconventional or "wild" they may seem.
2. Foster an environment of open-mindedness and creativity, emphasizing quantity over quality during the idea generation process. Defer judgment and allow ideas to flow freely, building upon each other to fuel innovation and creative problem-solving.

Rapid Prototyping for Iterative Innovation:

1. Select one of the ideas generated during the brainstorming session to prototype. Utilize materials readily available

to you, focusing on creating a tangible representation of your solution concept.

2. Remember that the prototype does not need to be perfect; the primary objective is to bring your idea to life in a physical form. Embrace imperfections and view the prototype as a tool for gathering feedback and iteration.

3. Solicit feedback from peers, colleagues, or potential users by sharing your prototype and seeking their input. Use their insights to refine and iterate on your solution, moving closer to a viable innovation that addresses the identified problem effectively.

Challenge For You:

Identify an everyday inconvenience. Apply the design thinking process to develop a solution. Start with empathy—truly understand the problem from the user's perspective. Prototype a simple solution and seek feedback. How does this process change your approach to problem-solving?

Conclusion:

Design thinking offers a structured yet flexible framework for innovation that prioritizes the human element in problem-solving. By exploring its principles, methodologies, and real-world applications, this chapter illuminates the path to creating meaningful, user-centric solutions. As we delve deeper into the intricacies of design thinking in subsequent sections, we equip ourselves with the knowledge and tools necessary for fostering creativity, empathy, and innovation in our entrepreneurial endeavors. Through empathy, collaboration, and iterative learning, design thinking empowers us to tackle complex challenges with innovative solutions that resonate on a human level.

4

Disruptive Innovation: Reshaping Industries, Creating Opportunities

"Do not wait for leaders; do it alone, person to person."
— Mother Teresa

As we navigate the ever-evolving business landscape, disruptive innovation stands out as a pivotal force that redefines the status quo, creating unparalleled opportunities for growth and transformation. This chapter ventures into the heart of disruptive innovation, dissecting its essence, uncovering its defining traits, and showcasing how it serves as both a challenge and an opportunity for organizations. Through a blend of theory, real-life examples, and strategic insights, we embark on a journey to understand how disruptive innovation can be harnessed to foster entrepreneurial success and industry transformation.

Opening Anecdote: Beyond Meat's Quest to Redefine the Meat Industry

Ethan Brown, the founder of Beyond Meat, embarked on a mission to revolutionize the food industry by creating plant-based meat alternatives. Despite facing skepticism from industry experts and logistical challenges in production, Brown remained steadfast in his vision. Through relentless experimentation and a commitment to sustainability, Beyond Meat developed innovative products that closely mimic the taste and texture of animal-based meats. Today, Beyond Meat is a leader in the plant-based food sector, challenging the status quo and reshaping the future of food.

Understanding Disruptive Innovation: A Paradigm Shift

Disruptive innovation, as conceptualized by Clay Christensen, signals a paradigm shift in how we perceive market dynamics and business strategies. It underscores the emergence of products, services, or business models that initially cater to a niche market but eventually ascend to disrupt established incumbents, often rendering traditional offerings obsolete. This transformative concept thrives on simplicity, affordability, and accessibility, gradually improving to meet the demands of a broader customer base.

Key Characteristics of Disruptive Innovation:

- **Accessibility and Affordability:** Disruptive innovations provide simpler, more cost-effective solutions that appeal to previously underserved or overlooked segments.
- **Incremental Evolution:** While they may start with mod-

est performance, these innovations evolve, eventually meeting or exceeding the standards of traditional offerings.

- **Market Transformation:** They possess the potential to redefine industry landscapes, challenging entrenched business models and creating new market paradigms.

Quick Thought:
At the heart of every disruptive innovation lies a simple truth: addressing overlooked needs can lead to revolutionary change.

Entrepreneurship in Action: Key Ingredients

- **Insightful Observation:** Identifying gaps in current market offerings can reveal opportunities for disruption.
- **Lean Agility:** The ability to quickly adapt and iterate based on user feedback and market response is crucial for nurturing a disruptive solution.
- **Persistent Vision:** Maintaining a clear vision amidst uncertainty and skepticism is vital for disruptive innovators.

Case Study: Netflix's Streaming Revolution

Background: Netflix, originally a DVD rental service, faced fierce competition from established video rental giants like Blockbuster. As technology evolved and consumer preferences shifted, Netflix recognized the need to adapt its business model to remain relevant in the digital age.

Challenge: Netflix confronted the challenge of competing against industry giants with extensive brick-and-mortar presence and loyal customer bases. The emergence of online streaming posed a threat to traditional rental stores, requiring Netflix to pivot its strategy to survive in a rapidly changing landscape.

Strategy: Netflix strategically transitioned from a DVD rental service to a subscription-based streaming platform, offering subscribers unlimited access to a vast library of movies and TV shows for a monthly fee. By embracing technological advancements and capitalizing on the growing popularity of internet streaming, Netflix aimed to provide consumers with an affordable, convenient entertainment solution.

Outcome: Netflix's bold move into the streaming market revolutionized the entertainment industry, paving the way for the decline of traditional rental stores like Blockbuster. The company's streaming platform not only offered unparalleled convenience to consumers but also disrupted established distribution models, reshaping how content is consumed worldwide.

Lesson: Netflix's success underscores the importance of embracing technological advancements to redefine industry standards. By recognizing shifting consumer preferences and leveraging innovative solutions, companies can adapt to evolving market dynamics and secure their position as industry leaders.

Case Study: Uber's Ride-Sharing Disruption

Background: Uber, a transportation technology company, sought to revolutionize urban transportation by simplifying the process of booking rides through a user-friendly mobile app.

Founded in 2009, Uber faced significant regulatory hurdles and resistance from traditional taxi services as it attempted to disrupt the transportation industry.

Idea: Uber's innovative idea centered on simplifying urban transportation by providing a convenient, on-demand ride-sharing service accessible through a mobile app. The company aimed to offer consumers an alternative to traditional taxis by leveraging technology to connect riders with drivers in real-time.

Obstacle: Uber encountered resistance from regulatory agencies and entrenched taxi services wary of the disruption posed by the ride-sharing model. Overcoming regulatory hurdles and addressing concerns regarding safety, pricing, and labor rights emerged as significant obstacles for the company.

Approach: Uber leveraged technology to enhance service convenience and efficiency, streamlining the process of booking rides and providing transparent pricing and driver ratings. The company also implemented innovative features like GPS tracking and cashless transactions to improve the overall user experience.

Impact: Uber's ride-sharing platform catalyzed a shift towards gig economy models, empowering individuals to earn income as independent contractors by providing transportation services. The company's disruptive approach transformed personal transportation, offering consumers a more convenient and cost-effective alternative to traditional taxis.

Pro Tip: Embrace the mindset of a disruptor by continuously seeking to understand the underserved

```
needs within your industry. Where there is
complacency, there lies opportunity.
```

Strategies for Embracing Disruptive Innovation

1. **Vigilant Market Observation:** Stay attuned to emerging trends and shifts in consumer behavior that signal opportunities for disruption.
2. **Cultivating a Disruptive Culture:** Foster an environment that encourages risk-taking, values innovation, and supports creative problem-solving.
3. **Strategic Partnerships:** Collaborate with startups and innovators to gain insights into new technologies and business models.
4. **Adaptability:** Remain flexible in your strategies and operations to swiftly respond to disruptive threats and opportunities.

Exercise: Uncover Disruptive Opportunities

Market Gap Analysis for Innovative Insights:

1. Choose a sector or industry that intrigues you and conduct thorough research to identify existing gaps or unmet needs within its current offerings. Delve into market trends, consumer preferences, and emerging technologies to inform your analysis.
2. Evaluate potential areas where disruptive innovation could address these identified gaps, challenging conventional norms and redefining industry standards. Consider

how your innovation could revolutionize the sector and create significant value for consumers or businesses.

Prototype Development for Conceptual Exploration:

1. Based on your findings from the market gap analysis, sketch a basic concept of a product or service that has the potential to serve as a disruptive innovation in the identified sector. Focus on capturing the essence of your idea, emphasizing key features or functionalities that differentiate it from existing offerings.

2. Leverage your creativity and imagination to visualize how your innovation could transform the industry landscape, solving pain points and meeting unmet needs in innovative ways. Embrace experimentation and exploration during the prototyping process, allowing your concept to evolve and refine over time.

Feedback Loop Creation for Iterative Refinement:

1. Develop a comprehensive plan for gathering initial feedback on your concept from potential users or industry experts. Identify relevant stakeholders who can provide valuable insights and perspectives on your innovation.

2. Outline specific methods and channels for soliciting feedback, such as surveys, focus groups, or interviews. Establish clear objectives and criteria for evaluating feedback, ensuring that it aligns with your innovation goals and vision.

3. Emphasize the importance of an iterative feedback loop, incorporating feedback into subsequent iterations of your

concept to drive continuous improvement and refinement. Foster an environment of openness and collaboration, inviting stakeholders to actively participate in shaping the evolution of your disruptive innovation.

Challenge For You:

Select an industry you're passionate about. Imagine a disruptive innovation that could significantly alter its landscape. Consider the steps you would need to take to bring this innovation from concept to reality, focusing on the initial target market and potential growth trajectory.

Conclusion:

Disruptive innovation has the power to reshape industries, redefine consumer expectations, and open new pathways for entrepreneurial success. By understanding its dynamics and embracing its potential, entrepreneurs and

5

Creative Problem Solving: The Engine of Innovation

"I never dreamed about success. I worked for it."
— Estée Lauder

I n the realm of entrepreneurship, where change is the only constant, creative problem solving emerges as a critical skill set, driving innovation, surmounting challenges, and seizing opportunities. This chapter delves into the essence of creative problem solving, underscoring its pivotal role in entrepreneurial ventures and outlining effective strategies to cultivate this invaluable mindset. Through illustrative examples and detailed case studies, we'll observe firsthand how businesses have leveraged creative problem-solving techniques to navigate obstacles and achieve remarkable triumphs.

Opening Anecdote: LEGO's Creative Rebuild

Facing near-bankruptcy in the early 2000s, LEGO had to rethink its strategy in the face of growing digital entertainment. By returning to its roots of creativity and play, LEGO innovated through new themes, interactive sets, and digital ventures. This pivot not only saved the company but also cemented its legacy as a beacon of creativity and resilience.

Creative Problem Solving: Beyond Traditional Boundaries

At its core, creative problem solving is a multifaceted approach that transcends conventional thinking, inviting diverse perspectives and harnessing creativity to unearth novel solutions to complex challenges. It empowers individuals to look beyond the obvious, challenge the status quo, and explore the uncharted to discover breakthrough solutions.

The Significance of Creative Problem Solving in Entrepreneurship:

Entrepreneurship is inherently fraught with uncertainty and hurdles. The ability to creatively solve problems not only enables entrepreneurs to adeptly navigate these challenges but also to uncover hidden opportunities, adapt to fluctuating markets, and carve unique pathways to success. It's the creative problem solvers who often lead the charge in differentiation, innovation, and competitive advantage.

The Process of Creative Problem Solving:

Creative problem solving encompasses a structured yet flexible methodology that promotes innovation and critical thinking:

1. **Identify and Define the Problem:** It begins with a clear understanding of the challenge at hand, requiring thorough information gathering and insightful problem definition.
2. **Generate Ideas:** This stage focuses on ideation, employing techniques like brainstorming and lateral thinking to foster a wealth of creative possibilities.
3. **Evaluate and Select Solutions:** Following ideation, it's critical to assess the feasibility and potential impact of generated ideas, selecting the most promising solutions for implementation.
4. **Develop Implementation Plans:** With a solution in hand, detailed planning ensues to outline the steps, resources, and timelines necessary for execution.
5. **Execute and Iterate:** Implementation is monitored for effectiveness, with continuous feedback loops ensuring the solution evolves and improves over time.

Quick Thought:
  Creative problem solving isn't just about finding a solution; it's about reimagining what's possible.

Entrepreneurship in Action: Key Ingredients

- **Open-minded Exploration:** Encourage curiosity and the exploration of diverse ideas and perspectives.
- **Resilience in Iteration:** Embrace the iterative nature of

creativity—each failure is a stepping stone to success.

- **Collaborative Synergy:** Foster teamwork and the exchange of ideas, believing that collective minds fuel innovation.

Case Study: Slack's Communication Revolution

Background: Slack, a messaging platform for teams, identified a need for improved workplace communication solutions in an era of increasing digital collaboration. Founded in 2013, Slack aimed to streamline communication processes and enhance productivity by offering a user-friendly platform that prioritized seamless integration and intuitive design.

Challenge: Slack faced the challenge of competing in a crowded market dominated by established players offering traditional communication tools like email and instant messaging. To differentiate itself, Slack needed to identify and address the inefficiencies inherent in existing communication platforms while also offering a solution that resonated with users.

Approach: Slack adopted a creative problem-solving approach, conducting extensive research to understand the pain points and preferences of potential users. By prioritizing user experience and seamless integration with existing tools and services, Slack developed a platform that addressed the shortcomings of traditional communication tools while offering innovative features to enhance collaboration.

Solution: Slack introduced a messaging platform that combined real-time messaging, file sharing, and integration with third-party applications in a single, intuitive interface. The platform's customizable channels, threaded conversations, and search functionality streamlined communication and facilitated information sharing within teams, improving collaboration and productivity.

Outcome: Slack's innovative approach to workplace communication revolutionized the way teams collaborate and communicate, gaining widespread adoption across industries. By focusing on user experience and seamless integration, Slack distinguished itself in a competitive market, becoming a leading platform for digital collaboration and productivity enhancement.

```
Pro Tip: Cultivate an Environment of Persistent
Curiosity: Encourage continuous questioning and
exploration within your team. A culture that
champions curiosity not only fuels creative
problem-solving but also builds a resilient
foundation for innovation. By fostering an
environment where every challenge is met with a "What
if?" or "Why not?" you open the door to
unconventional solutions and breakthroughs.
```

Strategies for Fostering Creative Problem Solving:

1. **Cultivate a Growth Mindset:** Encourage an environment where challenges are seen as opportunities for growth and innovation.
2. **Diversity and Inclusion:** Leverage diverse viewpoints to enrich the problem-solving process, recognizing that varied perspectives lead to more innovative solutions.
3. **Resource Allocation:** Dedicate time and resources to creative endeavors, providing the tools and space necessary

for exploration and experimentation.

Exercise: Cultivating Creative Solutions

Problem Reframing for Innovative Insights:

1. Choose a challenge or problem within your industry that you find compelling or intriguing. Challenge yourself to look at the problem from multiple angles and perspectives, questioning underlying assumptions and reframing it in novel ways.
2. Apply creative thinking techniques such as lateral thinking, mind mapping, or analogical reasoning to generate alternative interpretations and insights. Explore how reframing the problem can unlock new opportunities for innovative solutions and approaches.

Idea Generation Workshop for Unleashing Creativity:

1. Host a brainstorming session with colleagues or peers, inviting diverse perspectives and encouraging participation from all participants. Create a supportive environment where wild ideas are welcomed, and judgment is deferred to foster creativity and exploration.
2. Facilitate the brainstorming process by providing clear guidelines and objectives for generating ideas. Use prompts, visual aids, or interactive exercises to stimulate creativity and inspire out-of-the-box thinking. Encourage participants to build upon each other's ideas and explore unconventional solutions to the identified challenge.

Prototype and Feedback Loop for Iterative Development:

1. Develop a simple prototype or proof of concept based on the most promising ideas generated during the brainstorming session. Focus on creating a tangible representation of your solution that can be easily shared and tested with potential users or stakeholders.
2. Solicit feedback on your prototype from a diverse range of perspectives, including end-users, industry experts, and internal stakeholders. Establish clear criteria for evaluating feedback and iterate on your prototype based on the insights gathered.
3. Emphasize the importance of an iterative feedback loop, incorporating feedback into subsequent iterations of your prototype to refine and improve its functionality, usability, and overall effectiveness. Strive for continuous learning and improvement as you work towards developing innovative solutions to complex challenges in your industry.

Challenge For You:
Choose a pressing issue in your community or industry. Apply the creative problem-solving process, from problem identification to prototyping a solution. Reflect on how this approach alters your perspective on challenges and opportunities.

Conclusion:
Creative problem solving is the engine that powers entrepreneurial innovation, enabling individuals and organizations to overcome complex challenges and achieve significant breakthroughs. By embracing this dynamic approach,

entrepreneurs can unlock new opportunities, drive meaningful change, and secure a competitive edge in the ever-evolving business landscape. As we progress through this exploration of creativity and innovation, we invite you to join us in unlocking the full potential of creative problem solving in driving entrepreneurial success.

6

Cultivating a Culture of Innovation: The Heartbeat of Entrepreneurial Success

"Innovation requires an experimental mindset."
— Denise Coates

I n the dynamic world of entrepreneurship, innovation transcends individual creativity and the mere use of advanced technologies. At its core, innovation is deeply embedded in an organization's culture, cultivating an atmosphere where novel ideas are celebrated, risks are welcomed, and experimentation is the norm. This chapter unravels the essence of creating a culture of innovation, highlighting the critical elements that foster such an environment and outlining strategies to nurture and sustain this culture within entrepreneurial ventures. Through engaging narratives and insightful case studies, we will explore how various organizations have successfully embedded innovation into their cultural fabric, reaping significant benefits from their forward-thinking approaches.

Opening Anecdote: The 3M Post-It Note Evolution

Consider 3M's journey with the Post-it Note, a product born out of failure and serendipity. Initially deemed a flop, the adhesive technology found its purpose through internal experimentation and creative application, ultimately becoming an iconic symbol of innovation. This story exemplifies how fostering a culture that encourages curiosity and experimentation can lead to unexpected success.

The Crucial Role of Culture in Sparking Innovation

A culture steeped in innovation acts as a catalyst, propelling teams to challenge the conventional, think creatively, and contribute actively to the organization's evolutionary journey. It lays the groundwork for ongoing learning, collaborative efforts, and the pursuit of uncharted territories.

Foundations of an Innovative Culture:

1. **Open and Supportive Environment:** Innovation flourishes where there's open communication, seamless collaboration, and the free exchange of ideas. A safe space where voices are heard and experimentation is encouraged is essential for cultivating creativity.
2. **Leadership Support and Empowerment:** Effective leaders are the linchpins of an innovative culture. By providing resources, championing innovation, and setting an example of continual growth, leaders can galvanize

their teams towards inventive thinking and ownership of new initiatives.

3. **Celebrating Failure as a Learning Tool:** A hallmark of an innovative culture is the reframing of failure as a vital step towards success. This perspective encourages risk-taking, fosters resilience, and supports the iterative refinement of ideas.

4. **Encouraging Cross-Pollination:** Diverse teams bring a wealth of perspectives, sparking creativity and innovation. By promoting collaboration across various departments and specializations, organizations can unlock new insights and solutions.

Strategies to Cultivate an Innovation-Driven Culture:

- **Articulate a Clear Vision:** Establishing a compelling vision galvanizes collective efforts towards innovation, providing both direction and inspiration.
- **Promote a Growth Mindset:** Encourage an ethos where challenges are seen as opportunities for growth, emphasizing the value of curiosity, adaptability, and perseverance.
- **Foster Idea Generation:** Implement systems and processes that invite idea sharing and experimentation. Recognize and reward contributions to innovation, further motivating creative endeavors.

Quick Thought:
A culture of innovation isn't built overnight. It's a sustained effort that permeates every aspect of an

organization, turning challenges into springboards for growth.

Case Study: Google's 20% Time

Background: Google's innovative approach to employee empowerment, known as "20% Time," originated from the company's founders, Larry Page and Sergey Brin. Introduced in the early days of Google, this policy allows employees to allocate 20% of their work hours to pursue personal passion projects unrelated to their primary responsibilities.

Challenge: In a fast-paced and competitive tech industry, fostering a culture of innovation is essential for staying ahead of the curve. Google recognized the challenge of maintaining a creative and entrepreneurial spirit as the company grew, and sought to provide employees with the autonomy and freedom to explore their interests while contributing to the company's overall goals.

Approach: Google's 20% Time initiative was designed to encourage creativity, experimentation, and risk-taking among employees. By dedicating a portion of their work hours to pursue passion projects, employees were empowered to explore new ideas, technologies, and solutions outside the scope of their daily responsibilities. Google provided resources and support to help employees turn their passion projects into tangible innovations.

Solution: Google's 20% Time initiative has led to the development of several groundbreaking products and features, including Gmail, Google News, and AdSense. By giving employees the opportunity to pursue their interests and work on projects they are passionate about, Google has fostered a culture of innovation that continues to drive the company's success.

Outcome: Google's 20% Time policy has had a significant impact on the company's innovation ecosystem, resulting in the creation of numerous products and services that have shaped the digital landscape. By empowering employees to explore and innovate, Google has maintained its position as a leader in the tech industry and continues to push the boundaries of what is possible.

```
Pro Tip: Innovation thrives in environments that
balance freedom with focus. Encourage exploration but
ensure it aligns with your organization's broader
goals and values.
```

Exercise: Fostering Innovation in the Workplace

Idea Journaling for Creative Exploration:

1. Encourage team members to keep an "Idea Journal" for a designated period, such as a week or a month. Instruct them to jot down any thoughts, observations, or inspirations related to improving processes, products, or services within the organization.
2. Provide guidance on what types of ideas to record, emphasizing the importance of capturing both small, incremental improvements and bold, transformative concepts. En-

courage participants to be open-minded and exploratory in their journal entries, welcoming all ideas without judgment.

Idea Sharing Sessions for Collaborative Innovation:

1. Organize regular idea-sharing sessions, such as weekly or monthly forums, where employees have the opportunity to present and discuss ideas from their journals. Create a supportive environment where team members feel comfortable sharing their thoughts and receiving constructive feedback.
2. Facilitate the idea-sharing process by establishing clear guidelines and expectations for presentations. Encourage presenters to articulate their ideas clearly, provide context for their proposals, and explain potential benefits or impacts on the organization.
3. Foster a culture of open innovation and collaborative refinement by actively engaging participants in discussions about the presented ideas. Encourage brainstorming, debate, and exploration of potential synergies or enhancements to further develop and strengthen the proposed concepts.

Prototype Projects for Iterative Experimentation:

1. Identify promising ideas generated during idea-sharing sessions for further exploration through small-scale prototyping. Select ideas that have the potential to address pressing challenges or opportunities within the organization and align with strategic objectives.

2. Form cross-functional teams to work on prototype projects, leveraging diverse skills and perspectives to bring ideas to life. Provide resources, support, and guidance to help teams develop and execute their prototypes effectively.

3. Emphasize the importance of learning from real-world feedback and iteration during the prototyping process. Encourage teams to gather feedback from stakeholders, test their prototypes in relevant environments, and iterate based on insights gained to refine and improve their solutions.

Challenge For You:

Identify an area within your organization ripe for innovation. Implement a mini "innovation sprint" to explore new ideas, encouraging participation across all levels. Reflect on the process and outcomes, seeking insights to refine your approach to cultivating an innovation culture.

Conclusion:

Creating a culture of innovation is pivotal for entrepreneurial success, enabling organizations to navigate the complexities of the modern business landscape with agility and creativity. This chapter has laid out the foundational elements of such a culture, along with actionable strategies to foster and sustain innovation. By embracing these principles, leaders can transform their organizations into incubators of innovation, continuously evolving and achieving remarkable feats in their respective domains.

As we advance through this exploration of innovation, the subsequent chapters will delve deeper into the mechanisms and strategies that further enable organizations to harness the full spectrum of their creative potential, ensuring a lasting impact on their industry and beyond.

7

Open Innovation and Collaboration: Expanding Horizons in Entrepreneurship

"The most meaningful way to succeed is to help others succeed."
— Adam Grant

I n the contemporary landscape of entrepreneurship, where the pace of change accelerates and the scope of knowledge expands, the synergy between innovation and collaboration becomes increasingly crucial. This chapter delves into the realm of open innovation, a paradigm that champions the melding of external insights with internal prowess to catalyze breakthrough advancements. Through a tapestry of real-world narratives and analytical case studies, we'll explore how embracing the ethos of open innovation and fostering robust collaborations can significantly propel businesses forward, transcending traditional industry boundaries and ushering in a new era of competitive agility.

Opening Anecdote: Philips Lighting's Luminous Path

Philips Lighting's journey into open innovation exemplifies how collaboration with tech startups and academic institutions led to the development of pioneering lighting solutions. By embracing external collaborations, Philips not only advanced its product offerings but also redefined the lighting industry's landscape, illuminating the potential of open innovation to drive sector-wide transformation.

The Essence of Open Innovation

Gone are the days when innovation was confined within the walls of corporate R&D labs. Open innovation heralds a shift towards a more inclusive, boundary-spanning approach—welcoming ideas, technologies, and collaborations from the world at large. It's about recognizing that the wellspring of ingenuity lies not just within an organization but also beyond its borders, in the vast expanse of global intellect and creativity.

Benefits Unleashed by Open Innovation:

- **Diverse Insights:** Tapping into the global reservoir of knowledge brings a rich diversity of thought, driving the conception of groundbreaking solutions.
- **Agility and Speed:** By leveraging external expertise and resources, companies can accelerate the development and deployment of innovations, swiftly navigating the route from concept to commercialization.

- **Risk Distribution:** Open innovation allows for the sharing of both risks and rewards, distributing the investment in new ventures among a wider array of stakeholders and thereby mitigating individual exposure.
- **Market Expansion:** Collaborative ventures often open new channels and markets, broadening the reach of innovative products and services to previously untapped consumer segments.

Cultivating a Framework for Open Innovation and Collaboration

1. **Strategic Stakeholder Engagement:** Identifying and cultivating relationships with a spectrum of partners—be it startups, academia, industry mavens, or even consumers—sets the stage for a vibrant collaborative ecosystem.
2. **Constructing Collaborative Platforms:** The creation of innovation hubs, such as incubators or co-creation labs, fosters a conducive environment for shared ideation and development endeavors.
3. **Navigating IP Challenges:** Establishing clear protocols for intellectual property management ensures that collaborations are built on a foundation of trust and mutual respect, safeguarding the interests of all parties involved.

Quick Thought:

Open innovation is not just about outsourcing ideas; it's about creating a symbiotic ecosystem where knowledge flows freely, fostering mutual growth.

Case Study: IBM's Cognitive Colloquy

IBM's initiative to partner with universities represents a strategic effort to advance the frontiers of cognitive computing. This collaboration aimed to leverage the vast potential of academic research to significantly enhance the capabilities of IBM's Watson, an AI system designed to understand, reason, learn, and interact in human-like ways.

- **The Vision:** To establish a leading edge in cognitive computing by harnessing the innovative power of academic partnerships.
- **The Challenge:** Integrating diverse academic research into practical AI applications while maintaining a rapid pace of technological development.
- **The Strategy:** IBM fostered close collaborations with universities, offering resources and platforms like Watson for academic research. This approach enabled the direct application of cutting-edge research to enhance Watson's capabilities.
- **The Outcome:** The partnership led to accelerated developments in artificial intelligence, resulting in novel applications of cognitive computing across various industries.
- **The Insight:** IBM's case underscores the value of collaborative ventures between the tech industry and academia. Such partnerships can significantly shorten the innovation cycle, propelling technological advancements and establishing new benchmarks in AI.

Case Study: Tesla's Electric Ambition

Tesla, under the visionary leadership of Elon Musk, took a groundbreaking step towards promoting sustainable transportation by opening its patents to the world. This bold move was aimed at encouraging innovation in electric vehicle (EV) technology and infrastructure, thereby fostering an industry-wide push towards a more sustainable future.

- **The Vision:** To catalyze the global transition to sustainable transportation by removing barriers to EV innovation.
- **The Challenge:** Overcoming the traditional competitive patent strategy to foster a collaborative ecosystem in the EV industry.
- **The Approach:** Tesla made its patents available to anyone, under the premise that open innovation would lead to rapid advancements in EV technology and infrastructure. This approach aimed to stimulate competition but also cooperation, accelerating the pace of sustainable transportation solutions.
- **The Result:** Tesla's initiative stimulated global advancements in EV technology and the development of charging infrastructure, contributing to a significant increase in the adoption of electric vehicles worldwide.
- **The Reflection:** Tesla's strategy illustrates how sharing knowledge and fostering an open-source environment can spur industry-wide progress. By elevating the sector as a whole, Tesla not only supported its mission of accelerating the world's transition to sustainable energy but also positioned itself as a leader in the global movement towards cleaner transportation.

Strategies to Nourish an Open Innovation Ecosystem

- **Embrace External Engagements:** Actively seek and foster collaborations that align with your strategic goals, embracing the notion that external partnerships can be a potent source of innovation.
- **Foster a Collaborative Culture:** Cultivate an organizational mindset that values openness, encourages cross-pollination of ideas, and recognizes the contributions of external partners.
- **Prioritize Flexibility:** Remain adaptable, allowing for the evolution of partnerships and projects in response to new insights and opportunities.

Pro Tip: Leverage the power of diversity in your open innovation efforts. Diverse teams bring a wide array of perspectives and solutions to the table. Encourage your teams to engage with external partners from different industries, cultures, and backgrounds. This diversity not only enriches the innovation process but also enhances the potential for truly groundbreaking solutions that could redefine markets or create entirely new ones.

Exercise: Cultivating Collaborative Partnerships

Identify Potential Partners for Innovation:

1. Brainstorm a list of organizations, communities, or individuals operating outside your immediate industry but possessing expertise, resources, or perspectives relevant to your business challenges or goals.
2. Consider diverse sectors, such as academia, non-profit organizations, startups, or government agencies, that may offer unique insights or technologies that could complement your organization's capabilities.

Develop a Collaboration Proposal for Strategic Engagement:

1. Select one or more potential partners from your list and develop a detailed collaboration proposal outlining the objectives, scope, and potential benefits of partnering with each entity.
2. Tailor your proposals to align with the interests, goals, and expertise of the prospective partners, emphasizing mutual value creation, shared objectives, and clear pathways for collaboration.
3. Include specific project ideas, potential deliverables, resource commitments, and desired outcomes to provide a comprehensive framework for the proposed collaboration.

Initiate a Pilot Collaboration to Explore Opportunities:

1. Reach out to the selected partner(s) to initiate discussions

about potential collaboration opportunities based on your proposal(s). Express your organization's interest in exploring innovative partnerships and the value proposition of working together.

2. Propose a small-scale pilot project or initial collaboration initiative that allows both parties to test the waters and assess the feasibility, compatibility, and potential impact of working together.

3. Establish clear goals, expectations, and timelines for the pilot collaboration, as well as mechanisms for communication, feedback, and evaluation to ensure alignment and transparency throughout the partnership process.

Challenge For You:

Reflect on a current challenge your organization faces. Consider how open innovation and collaboration could offer a solution. Identify a potential external partner and outline a strategy for engagement that aims to harness collective expertise in addressing the challenge.

Conclusion:

In a world where knowledge is vast and varied, the path to innovation is increasingly collaborative. This chapter underscores the transformative power of open innovation and the strategic imperatives for cultivating a culture that embraces external collaboration. Through the lens of pioneering companies and actionable strategies, we've seen how open innovation can serve as a catalyst for growth, driving businesses to new heights of ingenuity and success.

As we progress further into the intricacies of innovation, we continue to explore the mechanisms and mindsets that enable organizations to thrive in an era of unprecedented change, underscoring the critical role of collaboration in achieving sustainable innovation and entrepreneurial excellence.

8

Innovation Metrics and Evaluation: Navigating the Impact of New Ventures

"Measure what is measurable, and make measurable what is not so."
— Galileo Galilei

I n the dynamic sphere of entrepreneurship, gauging the success and impact of innovation is not just beneficial— it's imperative. This chapter delves into the pivotal role of innovation metrics and evaluation in sculpting a landscape where groundbreaking ideas are not only born but are nurtured and quantifiably assessed. Through a comprehensive look at essential metrics, evaluation methods, and enlightening case studies, we'll unpack how businesses can systematically measure and amplify their innovation efforts, ensuring that their ventures not only soar but thrive on measurable success.

Opening Anecdote: Dyson's Iterative Excellence

Dyson's journey, marked by over 5,000 prototypes of its first vacuum cleaner, epitomizes the essence of measuring and iterating innovation. This relentless pursuit of improvement, driven by precise evaluation and feedback, led to a product that revolutionized an industry, demonstrating the power of commitment to innovation metrics and evaluation.

The Critical Role of Innovation Metrics

Innovation metrics illuminate the path of progress, offering tangible insights into the effectiveness and reach of an organization's inventive endeavors. These metrics serve as a compass, guiding decision-making, resource allocation, and strategic planning. Furthermore, they act as a bridge, conveying the value and progress of innovation initiatives to stakeholders, fostering an environment of transparency and accountability.

Pivotal Innovation Metrics:

- **Financial Performance:** Metrics such as ROI, revenue growth from new products, and cost reductions spotlight the financial health and profitability of innovation activities, exemplifying Apple's success through the financial triumphs of its product launches.
- **Customer Engagement:** Customer-centric metrics, including satisfaction scores and net promoter scores (NPS), offer insights into the market's reception of innovations, much like Amazon's relentless focus on customer feedback fuels its continuous evolution.
- **Operational Efficiency:** Indicators such as time to

market, idea-to-execution ratios, and innovation spend efficiency reflect the internal process's effectiveness, with Google's "20% time" showcasing how employee-led projects can yield substantial innovative output.

- **Intellectual Capital:** Metrics tracking patents filed, patents granted, and the strategic value of an IP portfolio underscore the creation and protection of novel ideas, as seen in IBM's robust IP management practices.

Frameworks for Innovation Evaluation:

- **Balanced Scorecard:** This strategic tool evaluates innovation from multiple facets—financial, customer, internal processes, and learning—offering a holistic view of innovation performance and strategic alignment.
- **Innovation Index:** A composite measure that amalgamates various innovation indicators into a singular score, providing a snapshot of an organization's innovation prowess, similar to GE's Innovation Barometer.
- **Benchmarking Analysis:** Comparing an organization's innovation metrics against peers and industry standards to identify competitive positioning and areas for improvement, a strategy that has kept Apple at the innovation forefront.

Quick Thought:
Innovation metrics are not just numbers; they're the narratives of progress, challenges, and triumphs in an organization's journey of creation and growth.

Case Study: Philips Lighting's Bright Ideas

Background: Formerly known as Philips Lighting and now operating as Signify, the company has been a trailblazer in leveraging open innovation to drive product development. Recognizing the value of collaboration and external partnerships, Philips Lighting has embraced a strategy that encourages sharing ideas and resources across organizational boundaries.

Challenge: In an increasingly competitive market, staying at the forefront of innovation is essential for Philips Lighting to maintain its market position and meet the evolving needs of customers. The challenge lies in fostering a culture of open innovation that enables the company to tap into external expertise and resources while effectively managing partnerships and collaborations.

Approach: Philips Lighting has adopted a multifaceted approach to open innovation, leveraging metrics such as partnerships forged, patents filed, and market share growth to measure the success of its collaborative efforts. By actively seeking partnerships with startups, research institutions, and other industry players, Philips Lighting has been able to access new technologies, insights, and market opportunities.

Solution: Through its open innovation initiatives, Philips Lighting has been able to bring a diverse range of perspectives and expertise into its product development process. By collaborating with external partners, the company has been able to accelerate the pace of innovation, introduce new products and solutions to the market, and strengthen its competitive position.

Outcome: Philips Lighting's commitment to open innovation has resulted in numerous successes, including the development of innovative lighting solutions that address the changing needs of customers and markets. By embracing collaboration and external partnerships, the company has been able to drive growth, expand its product portfolio, and maintain its leadership position in the lighting industry.

```
Pro Tip: Tailor your innovation metrics to reflect
your organization's unique goals and challenges.
While standard metrics provide a baseline, customized
metrics will capture the nuances of your innovation
journey, offering clearer insights and more
actionable data.
```

Strategies for Cultivating a Metrics-Driven Innovation Culture

- **Embed Metrics in Decision Making:** Integrate innovation metrics into strategic planning and decision-making processes to align innovation efforts with organizational goals.
- **Encourage a Learning Environment:** Promote an organizational culture that values data-driven insights, encourages experimentation, and views failures as opportunities for learning and growth.
- **Foster Transparency and Accountability:** Use metrics to communicate innovation progress and outcomes transparently, building trust and accountability within teams and with stakeholders.

Exercise: Driving Innovation through Metrics and Feedback

Metrics Identification Workshop for Innovation:

1. Facilitate a workshop with key stakeholders to identify the top three innovation metrics aligned with your organization's current objectives and strategic priorities.
2. Explore a range of potential metrics, such as idea generation rates, time-to-market for new products or services, customer satisfaction with innovative solutions, or revenue generated from new innovations.
3. Discuss how each metric can be effectively measured, tracked, and integrated into regular reporting processes to provide actionable insights and drive continuous improvement.

Innovation Audit for Performance Evaluation:

1. Conduct an innovation audit to evaluate recent projects or initiatives against the identified innovation metrics. Assess the impact, success, and effectiveness of each project in driving innovation within the organization.
2. Analyze the innovation performance of each project or initiative based on the selected metrics, identifying strengths, weaknesses, and areas for improvement.
3. Use the findings from the innovation audit to inform future decision-making, resource allocation, and strategic planning efforts, ensuring alignment with overall innovation goals and objectives.

Feedback Loop Implementation for Continuous Improvement:

1. Develop and implement a systematic approach for collecting feedback on innovation efforts, both internally from employees and externally from customers or other stakeholders.
2. Establish channels for gathering feedback, such as surveys, focus groups, suggestion boxes, or regular innovation forums, to capture insights, ideas, and suggestions for improvement.
3. Utilize the feedback collected to refine the chosen innovation metrics, adjust innovation strategies and initiatives, and drive continuous learning and improvement across the organization's innovation ecosystem.

Challenge For You:

Select an innovation project within your organization or a new idea you're exploring. Apply the discussed metrics to evaluate its potential impact, feasibility, and alignment with your strategic goals. Reflect on this process to enhance your approach to innovation measurement and evaluation.

Conclusion:

Innovation metrics and evaluation are indispensable tools in the entrepreneur's arsenal, enabling not just the tracking of progress but also the fostering of a culture that prizes data-driven insights and continuous improvement. By adopting a structured approach to innovation measurement, organizations can navigate the complexities of modern business with greater clarity and purpose. As we move forward, we'll delve deeper into strategies and practices that further refine our ability to harness innovation's full potential, driving sustainable growth and lasting success in the entrepreneurial landscape.

9

Innovation Leadership: Catalysts for Transformative Change

"A leader is best when people barely know he exists when his work is done, his aim fulfilled, they will say: we did it ourselves."
— *Lao Tzu*

At the heart of every trailblazing organization lies a core of visionary leadership that not only dreams of a future replete with innovation but also sets the wheels in motion to realize it. This chapter embarks on an insightful journey into the essence of innovation leadership, illuminating the crucial role leaders play in nurturing a culture ripe for creativity, empowering teams to reach their creative potential, and spearheading initiatives that break new ground. We dissect the attributes that distinguish innovative leaders and dive into compelling narratives of organizations propelled to new heights by such leadership.

Opening Anecdote: Leading with Vision: The Story of Barbara Corcoran

Barbara Corcoran, the real estate mogul and entrepreneur, faced a pivotal moment early in her career when she sought to establish her presence in the competitive New York City real estate market. Armed with a $1,000 loan, she founded The Corcoran Group, initially facing skepticism and rejection from established players in the industry. Undeterred, Corcoran relied on her innate ability to envision possibilities where others saw obstacles. She fostered a culture of innovation within her team, encouraging them to explore unconventional strategies and embrace calculated risks. Through her visionary leadership, Corcoran transformed The Corcoran Group into a real estate powerhouse, disrupting traditional practices and pioneering innovative marketing techniques that set new industry standards.

Innovation Leadership: The Keystone of Creative Endeavors

Innovation leadership transcends conventional leadership paradigms by emphasizing the creation of an environment where taking calculated risks, fostering original thinking, and championing continuous improvement are the norm. Leaders in this space don't just direct; they inspire, motivate, and provide the scaffolding for innovation to flourish.

Hallmarks of Innovative Leaders:

- **Visionary Insight:** Leaders like Elon Musk exemplify the ability to foresee and shape the future, guiding their organizations toward uncharted territories with unwavering conviction.

- **Adventurous Spirit:** Figures such as Jeff Bezos embody the essence of embracing risks as avenues for discovery, underscoring the importance of resilience in the face of setbacks.
- **Empowerment and Teamwork:** Leaders like Satya Nadella highlight the significance of nurturing a collaborative spirit, valuing diverse input, and empowering individuals to contribute fully to the organization's innovative pulse.
- **Perpetual Learners:** Sheryl Sandberg's advocacy for a culture steeped in continuous growth and learning exemplifies how leaders can foster an environment where curiosity and the quest for knowledge drive innovation forward.

Innovative Leadership in Action:

- **Cultivating Ideas:** Innovative leaders implement mechanisms such as Google's famed "20% time" to inspire idea generation and exploration, demonstrating a commitment to leveraging the collective creativity of their workforce.
- **Championing Diversity:** By assembling teams that mirror the world's rich tapestry, leaders like Tim Cook ensure that a broad spectrum of perspectives fuels the innovation engine.
- **Encouraging Bold Experiments:** Netflix's Reed Hastings represents the pinnacle of fostering a culture where experimentation is celebrated, and 'failures' are seen as milestones on the path to groundbreaking innovation.

- **Promoting Learning:** Sundar Pichai's leadership at Alphabet underscores the belief that a knowledgeable and curious workforce is the bedrock of continuous innovation.

Case Study: Apple's Renaissance under Steve Jobs

Background: Steve Jobs's return to Apple in the late 1990s marked a pivotal moment in the company's history. At the time, Apple was struggling, with declining sales and a lack of innovative products. Jobs's vision and leadership would ultimately lead to a renaissance for the company, transforming it into a powerhouse of innovation.

Challenge: Upon his return, Jobs faced significant challenges, including a fragmented product lineup, low morale among employees, and fierce competition from rivals such as Microsoft. The challenge was to revitalize Apple's product offerings, reignite innovation, and restore the company's reputation as a leader in the technology industry.

Approach: Jobs took a bold and decisive approach to address Apple's challenges. He streamlined the product lineup, focusing on a few key products that he believed had the potential to revolutionize the industry. He also instilled a culture of innovation within the company, empowering employees to think creatively and take risks.

Solution: Under Jobs's leadership, Apple launched a series of groundbreaking products, including the iMac, iPod, iPhone, and iPad. These products not only redefined their respective markets but also set new industry standards for design, functionality, and user experience. Jobs's uncompromising commitment to quality and innovation propelled Apple to unprecedented success.

Outcome: Apple's renaissance under Steve Jobs transformed the company into one of the most valuable and influential technology companies in the world. Jobs's vision, leadership, and relentless pursuit of innovation continue to shape Apple's identity and drive its success to this day.

Case Study: Pixar's Creative Empire

Background: Under the stewardship of Ed Catmull, Pixar became synonymous with creativity and innovation in the animation industry. Catmull's leadership and the company's collaborative culture would lead to a series of animated masterpieces that captivated audiences worldwide.

Challenge: When Catmull co-founded Pixar in 1986, the animation industry was dominated by traditional studios like Disney. The challenge for Pixar was to establish itself as a major player in the industry and create animated films that could compete with Disney's classics.

Approach: Catmull recognized the importance of fostering a culture of collaboration and creativity within Pixar. He encouraged open communication, risk-taking, and experimentation, allowing artists and filmmakers to push the boundaries of animation.

Solution: Through a combination of cutting-edge technology and storytelling prowess, Pixar produced a string of critically acclaimed and commercially successful films, including "Toy Story," "Finding Nemo," and "Up." These films not only showcased Pixar's technical innovation but also demonstrated its ability to connect with audiences on an emotional level.

Outcome: Pixar's creative empire has had a profound impact on the animation industry, inspiring filmmakers and artists around the world. Catmull's leadership and Pixar's collaborative culture continue to drive innovation and creativity, ensuring that the company remains at the forefront of animated filmmaking.

Case Study: Alibaba's E-commerce Revolution

Background: Jack Ma's vision for Alibaba was to create an interconnected trading platform that would empower millions of small and medium-sized enterprises (SMEs) in China and around the world. Through his leadership, Alibaba would reshape the digital commerce landscape and revolutionize the way business is conducted.

Challenge: When Ma founded Alibaba in 1999, e-commerce was still in its infancy in China. The challenge for Alibaba was to overcome skepticism and regulatory hurdles, as well as to build a platform that could effectively connect buyers and sellers in a vast and diverse market.

Approach: Ma's approach to building Alibaba was rooted in innovation and entrepreneurship. He leveraged technology to create user-friendly platforms like Taobao and Tmall, which enabled SMEs to reach customers and conduct business online. He also focused on building trust and credibility with both buyers and sellers, ensuring a positive user experience.

Solution: Alibaba's commitment to innovation and customer satisfaction would propel the company to become the largest e-commerce platform in the world. Through its various platforms and services, Alibaba has transformed the way businesses operate, facilitating billions of dollars in transactions and empowering millions of entrepreneurs.

Outcome: Alibaba's e-commerce revolution has had a profound impact on the global economy, enabling SMEs to thrive in an increasingly digital world. Ma's vision and leadership continue to drive Alibaba's success, ensuring that the company remains at the forefront of innovation and entrepreneurship.

```
Pro Tip: True innovation leadership involves not just
fostering an environment where creativity can thrive
but also actively participating in that creative
process. Innovative leaders don't just ask for new
ideas; they are often the ones rolling up their
sleeves to work alongside their teams to develop
those ideas into reality. They show that innovation
is not the responsibility of a select few within the
organization but a collective effort that requires
active engagement at all levels.
```

Strategies for Fostering Innovative Leadership:

- **Lead by Example:** Embody the innovation you wish to see in your organization. Your actions set a powerful precedent for your team's exploratory journey.
- **Foster an Inclusive Culture:** Create an environment where every voice can be heard and every idea has the potential to be a game-changer.
- **Embrace and Share Failures:** Normalize setbacks as essential components of the innovation process, sharing lessons learned to demystify risk-taking.
- **Invest in Your Team:** Provide opportunities for professional growth and learning, recognizing that an empow-

ered team is your greatest asset in navigating the innovation landscape.

Exercise: Cultivating a Culture of Innovation

Reflective Leadership Analysis for Innovation:

1. Take time to introspect and assess your leadership style in relation to fostering innovation within your team or organization.
2. Identify aspects of your leadership style that currently support innovation and areas that may require further development or growth.
3. Reflect on how you can adapt and shift your leadership approach to more actively encourage creativity, experimentation, and risk-taking among your team members.

Diversity Audit for Innovation Enhancement:

1. Conduct a comprehensive audit of your team or organization's current diversity and inclusion practices, focusing on how diverse perspectives are represented and valued.
2. Evaluate the effectiveness of existing diversity initiatives and identify any gaps or areas for improvement in fostering an inclusive culture that embraces diverse voices and experiences.
3. Develop a strategic plan to enhance diversity and inclusion efforts, recognizing the critical role they play in driving innovation and creativity within the organization.

Innovation Feedback Loop Implementation:

1. Establish a structured feedback mechanism to capture innovative ideas and suggestions from team members on a regular basis.
2. Choose a suitable platform or format for gathering feedback, such as monthly innovation meetings, digital suggestion boxes, or dedicated innovation workshops.
3. Encourage active participation and engagement from team members, ensuring that all ideas are heard, valued, and explored to fuel continuous innovation and improvement within the organization.

Challenge For You:

Identify a project or initiative within your organization that has been stagnant or faced challenges. Apply the principles of innovation leadership to this scenario. How might a shift in leadership approach or team dynamics spark new life into the project? Develop a small-scale action plan to test your hypothesis.

Conclusion:

Innovation leadership is not merely about directing from the sidelines; it's about embedding oneself in the very fabric of the innovation process, championing creativity, encouraging risk-taking, and leading by example. Through this chapter, we've explored the multifaceted role of leadership in innovation, the characteristics that define innovative leaders, and the practices that can help cultivate a robust culture of innovation. The real-life examples and strategies discussed provide a roadmap for aspiring leaders to inspire and drive innovation within their teams and organizations. As we move forward, the insights gained here will serve as a foundation for developing and refining leadership approaches that not only embrace but actively drive innovation.

10

Ethical Considerations in Innovation: Navigating the Moral Compass

"Ethics is knowing the difference between what you have a right to do and what is right to do."
— Potter Stewart

I n the ever-accelerating race towards innovation, the importance of anchoring initiatives in ethical consider- ations cannot be overstated. This chapter embarks on a critical exploration of how ethical frameworks can guide innovation towards not only being groundbreaking but also socially responsible and beneficial. Through examining the ethical dilemmas faced by leading companies and outlining best practices for ethical innovation, we aim to illuminate the path for organizations striving to balance ambitious technological advancements with the imperatives of moral responsibility.

Opening Anecdote: The Theranos Cautionary Tale

Theranos's story serves as a stark reminder of the repercussions when ethical considerations are sidelined in the rush to innovate. The company's fall from grace underscored the critical need for transparency, accountability, and the prioritization of patient safety over corporate ambitions, highlighting the dire consequences of ethical lapses in innovation.

The Imperative of Ethical Considerations in Innovation

Ethics in innovation acts as a beacon, ensuring that the relentless pursuit of progress remains aligned with principles of integrity, fairness, and social good. It prompts organizations to weigh the consequences of their innovations, ensuring that advancements are made responsibly, with consideration for all stakeholders involved.

Striking a Balance: Ethical Dimensions of Innovation

- **Consumer Protection and Well-being:** The commitment to consumer safety and welfare is paramount, requiring rigorous evaluation of products and services to safeguard against harm.
- **Data Integrity and Privacy:** As digital innovation continues to evolve, the stewardship of personal data demands stringent measures to protect privacy and ensure security against breaches.
- **Environmental Stewardship:** Innovators bear the responsibility to minimize ecological footprints, championing sustainability as an integral part of the innovation lifecycle.

- **Social Equity and Accessibility:** Ensuring innovations contribute to bridging societal gaps rather than widening them is a critical ethical concern, calling for inclusive and equitable approaches to innovation.

Frameworks for Upholding Ethical Standards in Innovation

- **Ethical Impact Assessments:** A systematic approach to preemptively identifying and mitigating potential ethical risks, ensuring innovations contribute positively to society and do not inadvertently cause harm.
- **Adherence to Ethical Codes:** Establishing and following a set of ethical guidelines that dictate the conduct of innovation processes, setting clear expectations for ethical behavior and decision-making.

> *Quick Thought:*
>
> *Ethical innovation is not a constraint but a catalyst for deeper, more meaningful progress that genuinely enhances lives and respects our shared social fabric.*

Case Study: Tesla's Sustainability Drive

Background: Tesla, under the leadership of Elon Musk, has become synonymous with innovation in the electric vehicle (EV) and renewable energy sectors. Musk's vision for Tesla goes beyond just creating stylish electric cars; it encompasses a commitment to sustainability and ecological responsibility.

Challenge: When Tesla first entered the automotive industry, skeptics doubted the feasibility and market demand for electric vehicles. The challenge for Tesla was to overcome these doubts and establish itself as a leader in the EV market while promoting sustainable transportation solutions.

Approach: Musk's approach to sustainability at Tesla involves a holistic strategy that encompasses not only the development of electric vehicles but also renewable energy solutions such as solar panels and energy storage systems. Tesla's Gigafactories, which produce batteries for its vehicles and energy products, are powered by renewable energy sources, further reducing the company's carbon footprint.

Solution: Through relentless innovation and a focus on quality and performance, Tesla has successfully positioned itself as a leader in the EV market. The company's electric vehicles, such as the Model S, Model 3, Model X, and Model Y, offer industry-leading range, performance, and safety features, attracting a growing number of consumers worldwide.

Outcome: Tesla's sustainability drive has had a profound impact on the automotive industry, inspiring other manufacturers to invest in electric vehicle technology and renewable energy solutions. Musk's vision for a sustainable future continues to drive innovation at Tesla, ensuring that the company remains at the forefront of environmental responsibility.

Case Study: Google's AI Principles

Background: Google, as a leading technology company, is at the forefront of artificial intelligence (AI) development. Recognizing the ethical implications of AI, Google has developed a set of principles to guide the responsible development and application of AI technologies.

Challenge: As AI technologies become increasingly integrated into various aspects of daily life, concerns about privacy, security, and fairness have emerged. The challenge for Google was to address these concerns and develop ethical guidelines that promote transparency, accountability, and user trust.

Approach: Google's approach to addressing the ethical challenges of AI involves collaboration with experts, stakeholders, and policymakers to develop comprehensive guidelines that reflect the company's values and commitments. The principles emphasize the importance of fairness, privacy, and accountability in AI development and deployment.

Solution: By proactively addressing ethical considerations, Google has demonstrated its commitment to responsible AI innovation. The company's AI principles serve as a framework for ensuring that AI technologies are developed and used in ways that benefit society while minimizing potential risks and harms.

Outcome: Google's AI principles have set a precedent for ethical AI development and application in the technology industry. By promoting transparency, accountability, and user trust, Google is helping to build public confidence in AI technologies and ensure that they are used responsibly for the benefit of all.

Pro Tip: Foster an ethical dialogue within your organization. Encourage open discussions about the ethical implications of innovation projects from the outset, ensuring a shared understanding and

```
commitment to ethical principles across all levels of
the organization.
```

Exercise: Ethical Innovation Framework

Ethical Scenario Analysis:

1. Select a current project or initiative within your organization and analyze it for potential ethical challenges it may encounter.
2. Discuss and brainstorm possible solutions or approaches to address these ethical dilemmas while ensuring alignment with ethical innovation principles.
3. Consider factors such as consumer safety, data privacy, environmental impact, and social equity in your analysis and solution development process.

Develop Your Ethical Guidelines:

1. Create a comprehensive set of ethical guidelines specifically tailored to your organization's innovation process.
2. Define clear principles and standards that prioritize ethical considerations throughout the entire innovation lifecycle.
3. Incorporate feedback and insights from diverse stakeholders to ensure that your ethical guidelines are robust, practical, and reflective of your organization's values and commitments.

Stakeholder Mapping for Ethical Impact Assessment:

1. Conduct a stakeholder mapping exercise for your next innovation project to identify all parties potentially impacted by the innovation.
2. Evaluate how the project could affect each stakeholder group positively or negatively, considering their interests, concerns, and values.
3. Develop strategies to engage with stakeholders, gather feedback, and address any ethical concerns or risks identified during the mapping process.

Challenge for You:

Reflect on an innovation in your field that has faced ethical scrutiny. Considering what you've learned, outline an alternative approach that balances innovative ambitions with ethical responsibilities. How could this alternative approach have mitigated ethical concerns while still achieving its goals?

Conclusion:

Ethical considerations form the cornerstone of sustainable and responsible innovation. By weaving ethical principles into the fabric of the innovation process, organizations can ensure their advancements serve not just the interests of shareholders but the well-being of all stakeholders and the broader community. As we venture further into the realms of innovation, the lessons and frameworks discussed in this chapter provide a moral compass to navigate the complex ethical landscapes we face, ensuring that our innovations lead us towards a future that is not only technologically advanced but also ethically sound and socially responsible.

11

Managing Innovation Processes: From Spark to Success

"Man cannot discover new oceans unless he has the courage to lose sight of the shore."
— André Gide

I nnovation is not merely a burst of creativity but a comprehensive journey that requires meticulous management from the initial spark of an idea to its full-fledged realization in the market. This chapter dives into the intricacies of managing innovation processes, laying out a roadmap for transforming creative concepts into tangible, successful innovations. Through the lens of proven principles, adaptable strategies, and inspirational real-world examples, we uncover the blueprint for navigating the innovation journey within the dynamic environment of entrepreneurial ventures.

Opening Anecdote: Pixar's Creative Resurgence

Pixar's journey from near obscurity to becoming a beacon of creativity in animation underscores the essence of managing innovation processes. Under the visionary leadership of Ed Catmull and John Lasseter, Pixar harnessed the power of storytelling and cutting-edge technology, navigating through challenges and leveraging collaborative creativity to produce hits like "Toy Story," which revolutionized the animation industry.

The Structured Pathway of Innovation Management

The innovation process is a multi-stage odyssey that demands thoughtful navigation through its various phases:

1. **Idea Generation:** The genesis of innovation lies in the cultivation of ideas. This fertile ground is nurtured through brainstorming, open dialogue with customers, and leveraging insights from diverse teams.
2. **Idea Evaluation:** Critical scrutiny follows, where ideas are assessed for their viability, market potential, and strategic fit, employing tools like feasibility studies and market analysis to sift the gold from the dross.
3. **Concept Development:** Promising ideas evolve into concrete concepts, undergoing meticulous refinement and prototyping to hone their market relevance and operational feasibility.
4. **Resource Allocation:** Strategic deployment of resources—capital, talent, and time—ensures that chosen concepts have the support necessary to burgeon into viable innovations.

5. **Implementation:** The rubber meets the road in this phase, as concepts are actualized through disciplined project management, embodying the innovation in a product, service, or process ready for the market.
6. **Testing and Iteration:** The initial market introduction brings valuable feedback, initiating cycles of refinement to perfect the offering based on real-world usage and customer insights.
7. **Scaling and Commercialization:** With a proven and polished innovation, the focus shifts to broadening its impact through strategic scaling and targeted market penetration efforts.

Quick Thought:

Effective innovation management harmonizes creativity with strategic execution, ensuring that visionary ideas achieve their transformative potential.

Strategies for Navigating the Innovation Journey

- **Fostering a Creative Culture:** Cultivating an environment that encourages risk-taking and values diversity of thought is foundational to generating a robust pipeline of innovative ideas.
- **Emphasizing Agile Methodologies:** Adopting flexible, iterative approaches to project management enables organizations to adapt swiftly to feedback and evolving market conditions, enhancing the resilience of the innovation process.

- **Prioritizing Cross-Functional Collaboration:** Breaking down silos and fostering interdisciplinary teams enrich the innovation journey with a multiplicity of perspectives, driving more holistic and impactful solutions.

Case Study: Procter & Gamble's Connect + Develop

Procter & Gamble (P&G), a multinational consumer goods corporation, embarked on a transformative journey with its Connect + Develop program, aiming to redefine the landscape of product development. Recognizing that great ideas and innovations can emerge from anywhere, not solely within the confines of the company, P&G sought to transcend the limitations of traditional research and development (R&D) models. This initiative represented a strategic pivot towards an open innovation paradigm, inviting a global network of thinkers - from entrepreneurs to inventors and beyond - to contribute to P&G's innovation ecosystem.

The Vision: P&G aimed to revolutionize its product development process by incorporating external ideas and innovations, acknowledging that significant inventions can come from any source, not just within the company.

The Challenge: Transforming the traditional, internally focused R&D model to a more open, collaborative approach without compromising on quality or increasing time-to-market for new products.

The Strategy: Launching the Connect + Develop program, P&G invited entrepreneurs, inventors, and other companies to submit their ideas for potential collaboration, effectively doubling its R&D capabilities through external partnerships.

The Impact: The initiative has led to numerous successful products, such as the Swiffer and Crest Whitestrips, significantly boosting P&G's innovation output and establishing it as a leader in consumer goods innovation through open collaboration.

Case Study: Amazon's Culture of Experimentation

At the heart of Amazon's meteoric rise and continued dominance in the digital marketplace is its foundational culture of experimentation. Spearheaded by founder Jeff Bezos, this ethos champions continuous innovation and customer-centricity through unabated exploration and embracing of new ideas. Amazon's operational model is built around the principle that fostering an environment where experimentation is encouraged at all levels ensures the company remains at the forefront of customer service, technology, and product offerings. This commitment to innovation through experimentation has cemented Amazon's status as a global leader, constantly pushing the boundaries of what is possible in the digital age.

The Vision: Amazon's founder, Jeff Bezos, championed a culture of innovation through relentless experimentation, aiming to make Amazon the earth's most customer-centric company by continuously exploring new ideas and technologies to enhance the customer experience.

The Challenge: Maintaining a balance between rapid innovation and operational efficiency in a sprawling global enterprise, ensuring that the experimentation culture does not lead to resource dilution or distract from the company's core objectives.

The Strategy: Encouraging small-scale experiments across the company, allowing teams the autonomy to pursue inno-

81

vative projects with a 'two-pizza team' concept (teams small enough to be fed with two pizzas), and embracing a 'fail fast, learn faster' philosophy to quickly iterate or pivot based on experiment outcomes.

The Impact: This approach has led to groundbreaking services like Amazon Prime, AWS, and Amazon Go, significantly enhancing Amazon's market leadership and disrupting multiple industries. Amazon's commitment to experimentation has not only fueled its rapid growth and diversification but also embedded innovation into the company's DNA, making it a standard-bearer for how large corporations can innovate at scale.

```
Pro Tip: Integrate feedback mechanisms at every stage
of the innovation process. Continual input from
customers, team members, and stakeholders is
invaluable in steering innovations towards success
and ensuring they remain aligned with market needs
and expectations.
```

Exercise: Innovation Workshop Series

Idea Generation Workshop:

1. Identify a pressing challenge or opportunity currently facing your organization.
2. Organize a dedicated workshop session focused on generating innovative solutions to address this challenge.
3. Encourage open and unrestricted brainstorming, inviting

diverse perspectives and insights from team members across different departments or functions.

Concept Viability Assessment:

1. Select one promising idea generated during the workshop for further evaluation.
2. Develop a set of criteria to assess the idea's feasibility, market potential, and alignment with your organization's strategic goals.
3. Conduct a comprehensive assessment, considering factors such as resource requirements, market demand, competitive landscape, and potential risks.

Prototype Development Challenge:

1. Choose the idea with the highest viability score and initiate a small-scale prototype development project.
2. Develop an agile project plan with clear milestones and timelines for prototype iteration and refinement.
3. Gather feedback from potential users or stakeholders throughout the prototype development process, prioritizing agility and responsiveness to insights gathered for continuous improvement.

Challenge for You:
Select a project or initiative within your organization that has not reached its full potential. Apply the principles of effective innovation management discussed in this chapter to reinvigorate the project. Document the process, challenges

encountered, and lessons learned, reflecting on how these insights can inform future innovation efforts.

Conclusion:

Managing innovation processes is an art and science, requiring a delicate balance between fostering creativity and executing with precision. This chapter has provided a comprehensive overview of the stages of innovation management, accompanied by strategies, real-world examples, and actionable insights to guide entrepreneurs and leaders. As we delve deeper into the facets of innovation in subsequent chapters, the principles and practices outlined here will serve as a cornerstone for cultivating a robust innovation ecosystem capable of driving sustained growth and success.

12

Intellectual Property and Innovation: Securing the Foundations of Creativity

"Intellectual property has the shelf life of a banana."
— Bill Gates

At the intersection of creativity and commerce lies the crucial domain of intellectual property (IP), serving as both the bedrock and the bulwark of innovation. This chapter delves into the intricate relationship between intellectual property and the dynamism of innovation, illustrating how the strategic management of IP assets underpins the successful transformation of visionary ideas into market-defining realities. Through an exploration of IP's various forms, its pivotal role in the innovation landscape, and strategic insights for IP management, complemented by illustrative case studies, we underscore the indispensable value of intellectual property in nurturing and sustaining the competitive edge of entrepreneurial ventures.

Opening Anecdote: The Missed Opportunity: Xerox PARC's Legacy

The story of Xerox PARC vividly captures the essence of intellectual property's critical role in innovation. In the 1970s, PARC developed groundbreaking technologies, including the graphical user interface (GUI), that would later become foundational to personal computing. However, Xerox failed to capitalize on these innovations, allowing other companies like Apple to leverage similar ideas to transform the industry. This tale underscores the importance of not only fostering innovation but also securing and strategically managing intellectual property to fully reap its benefits.

The Spectrum of Intellectual Property

Intellectual property stands as the guardian of creativity, offering a suite of protections that encapsulate the breadth of human ingenuity:

- **Patents:** The lifeblood of technological progress, patents protect the novel functionalities and processes that push industries forward, offering inventors exclusive rights as a reward for their contributions to the public knowledge base.
- **Copyrights:** The muse of the arts and letters, copyright safeguards the expressions of ideas, ensuring that creators can share their works without fear of unauthorized replication.
- **Trademarks:** The sentinels of identity in the marketplace, trademarks defend the symbols and names that signify quality and origin, building trust and loyalty among con-

sumers.

- **Trade Secrets:** The unseen advantage in the competitive arena, trade secrets secure proprietary knowledge from prying eyes, preserving the unique aspects that differentiate one enterprise from another.

Intellectual Property: The Catalyst of Innovation

Intellectual property does not merely protect; it propels the mechanisms of innovation by:

- **Incentivizing Research and Development:** IP rights provide a framework within which inventors and creators can safely invest in innovation, assured by the knowledge that their discoveries and creations will be protected.
- **Enabling Collaborative Endeavors:** By defining clear boundaries of ownership and control, IP rights facilitate partnerships and collaborations that might otherwise be fraught with uncertainty.
- **Safeguarding Competitive Advantage:** Intellectual property rights offer a legal recourse to defend against imitators, ensuring that innovators can reap the rewards of their pioneering efforts.

Strategic Management of Intellectual Property

Effectively navigating the IP landscape requires a deliberate strategy, encompassing:

- **Thorough IP Audits:** A comprehensive inventory of IP assets allows organizations to fully understand and leverage their portfolio for strategic advantage.
- **Adaptive IP Strategies:** Tailoring IP protection and

enforcement strategies to align with business objectives and market realities ensures the optimal deployment of resources.

- **Vigilant Monitoring and Enforcement:** Proactively defending IP rights against infringement is critical to maintaining the integrity and value of the IP portfolio.

> *Quick Thought:*
> *Intellectual property is the invisible yet formidable backbone of innovation, ensuring that creativity is both protected and rewarded, fostering a cycle of continuous innovation.*

Entrepreneurship in Action: Key Ingredients

- **Strategic IP Evaluation:** Successful innovators understand the importance of regularly assessing their IP portfolio to identify opportunities for protection, licensing, or development.
- **Proactive IP Education:** Entrepreneurs and innovators prioritize educating their teams about the value of IP, ensuring that everyone understands how to safeguard and respect these assets.
- **IP as a Business Asset:** Leading companies view their IP not just as legal protection but as a core component of their business strategy, influencing product development, marketing, and competitive positioning.

Case Study: Apple's Design Patents

Apple's defense of its design patents, particularly in high-profile legal battles over smartphone features, underscores the significance of protecting innovative design elements that define brand identity and consumer experience.

- **The Vision:** To safeguard the distinctive aesthetic and functional design elements that set its products apart.
- **The Challenge:** Navigating complex legal landscapes to defend against infringements that dilute brand value and consumer perception.
- **The Strategy:** Vigorous enforcement of design patents through litigation and negotiation to deter infringement and maintain market leadership.
- **The Impact:** Apple's IP strategy has not only protected its innovations but also reinforced its position as a leader in design-driven technology innovation.

Case Study: Pfizer's Patent Strategy for Viagra:

Pfizer's management of Viagra's patent life cycle showcases the strategic use of IP to extend market exclusivity and maximize the commercial lifecycle of pharmaceutical innovations.

- **The Vision:** To maximize the commercial potential of Viagra while navigating the patent expiration landscape.
- **The Challenge:** Contending with the impending expiration of key patents and the threat of generic competition.
- **The Strategy:** Employing strategic patent extensions, litigation, and alternative formulations to prolong market

exclusivity.

- **The Impact:** Pfizer successfully extended Viagra's market dominance, significantly impacting its revenue stream and setting a precedent for pharmaceutical IP management.

```
Pro Tip: Prioritize Strategic IP Planning Early:
Engage in intellectual property planning from the
inception of your ideas. Early and strategic
consideration of IP not only secures your innovations
but also positions your venture for sustainable
growth and competitive advantage. Understand the
types of IP relevant to your business and integrate
IP management as a core element of your business
strategy, ensuring that your creative foundations are
both protected and leveraged effectively.
```

Exercise: Intellectual Property (IP) Strategy Workshop

IP Audit Challenge:

1. Conduct a comprehensive audit of your personal or company's intellectual property assets.
2. Identify any innovations, inventions, or creative works that are currently unsecured or inadequately protected.
3. Outline a strategic plan to safeguard these assets, including steps for patenting, copyrighting, trademarking, or establishing trade secret protections.

IP Strategy Plan:

1. Select a hypothetical product or service from your industry or area of interest.
2. Draft a simple yet effective intellectual property strategy tailored to this product or service.
3. Consider the appropriate mix of IP protections, including patents, copyrights, trademarks, and trade secrets, to safeguard your innovation and maximize its market potential.

Competitive Analysis:

1. Choose a direct competitor or industry leader known for their innovative products or services.
2. Analyze their IP strategy, including the types of intellectual property they protect and the methods they employ for protection.
3. Identify potential areas of overlap or differentiation between your IP strategy and theirs, and explore opportunities for strategic alignment or competitive advantage.

Challenge For You:

Identify a project or initiative within your organization that could benefit from a stronger focus on intellectual property. Consider how enhancing your IP strategy could improve innovation outcomes, protect your creations, or generate additional revenue streams. Develop a plan to integrate these IP considerations into the project's development process.

Conclusion:

Intellectual property is a vital component of the innovation ecosystem. It incentivizes innovation, facilitates collaboration, protects market share, and attracts investment. Effective management of intellectual property assets is crucial for leveraging their value and ensuring their protection. In this chapter, we explored the different types of intellectual property, their role in fostering innovation, and strategies for managing intellectual property assets. Real-life examples, such as Coca-Cola's trademark protection, illustrate the significance of intellectual property in driving business success through innovation. By understanding and effectively managing intellectual property, entrepreneurs can safeguard their innovations, nurture a culture of innovation, and gain a competitive edge in the dynamic business landscape.

13

Innovation in Marketing and Customer Experience: Crafting Connections

"A brand is the set of expectations, memories, stories, and relationships that, taken together, account for a consumer's decision to choose one product or service over another."
— Seth Godin

Today's market landscape demands more than just delivering products and services; it requires creating resonant experiences and meaningful connections with customers. This chapter unfolds the synergy between innovation, marketing, and customer experience, showcasing how businesses can wield this power to captivate, engage, and retain customers. Through a blend of modern marketing strategies and a relentless focus on customer-centricity, companies like Amazon and Netflix have redefined engagement, setting new benchmarks in brand loyalty. We explore these dynamics, underpinned by real-life success stories, offering a blueprint for embedding innovation into the marketing DNA of businesses.

Opening Anecdote: Embracing Authenticity: Dove's Beauty Revolution

The transformation of Dove from a traditional beauty soap to a brand synonymous with real beauty and self-esteem illustrates the profound impact of innovative marketing. Dove's "Real Beauty" campaign, a radical departure from industry norms, not only sparked conversations around beauty stereotypes but also deeply resonated with women worldwide, significantly boosting Dove's market presence and brand perception.

> *Quick Thought:*
>   *At the heart of innovative marketing lies the art of seeing the world through the customers' eyes, understanding their desires and dreams, and crafting experiences that echo those insights.*

Entrepreneurship in Action: Key Ingredients

- **Data-Driven Personalization:** Utilizing customer data to tailor marketing efforts and create personalized experiences, thereby enhancing engagement and loyalty.
- **Creating Immersive Experiences:** Leveraging technology to design experiential marketing that transcends traditional advertising, offering customers a vivid brand

encounter.

- **Authentic Engagement:** Building genuine relationships with customers through transparent communication and meaningful interactions, fostering trust and advocacy.

Case Study: Spotify's Personalized Playlists

Spotify embarked on a mission to redefine the music listening experience, envisioning a future where every user's interaction with music is as unique as their own personal taste. In a digital era overflowing with music choices, Spotify recognized the need to distinguish itself by curating personalized listening experiences that resonate on an individual level. This vision led to the creation of features like "Discover Weekly," a paradigm shift in music streaming that leverages sophisticated algorithms and deep user data analytics to craft playlists tailored to each listener's preferences and historical listening habits.

The Vision: To revolutionize music listening by offering highly personalized music experiences to its users, making every interaction uniquely tailored.

The Challenge: Amidst the vast sea of digital music, Spotify aimed to stand out by delivering personalized content that resonates with individual tastes and preferences.

The Strategy: Leveraging sophisticated algorithms and user data analytics, Spotify introduced personalized playlists, such as "Discover Weekly," that curate songs based on each user's listening history and preferences.

The Impact: This innovative approach not only elevated the user experience but also solidified Spotify's position as a leader in the music streaming industry, significantly increasing user engagement and subscription rates.

Case Study: Zappos' Customer Service Excellence

Zappos, an online shoe and clothing retailer, set out with the ambitious goal of revolutionizing the online shopping experience through unparalleled customer service. Understanding the inherently impersonal nature of e-commerce, Zappos aimed to build trust and forge lasting relationships with customers by prioritizing their satisfaction above all else. This commitment was manifested in various strategic initiatives, including extensive customer service training for employees, empowering staff to make decisions that benefit the customer, and offering a generous 365-day return policy. These efforts collectively transformed Zappos into an emblem of customer service excellence, redefining expectations for e-commerce platforms and cultivating a loyal customer base.

The Vision: Zappos sought to redefine the online shopping experience by prioritizing customer service above all else, aiming to create lasting relationships with customers.

The Challenge: In the impersonal realm of e-commerce, establishing a deep, trust-based connection with customers presented a significant challenge.

The Strategy: Implementing a customer-first philosophy, Zappos invested in extensive customer service training, empowered employees to go the extra mile, and introduced a 365-day return policy.

The Impact: This commitment to customer satisfaction transformed Zappos into a benchmark for exceptional customer service, fostering strong customer loyalty and setting a new standard in e-commerce.

```
Pro Tip: Embrace failure as a stepping stone to
innovation. Innovative marketing is experimental by
nature, and not all initiatives will succeed. View
each attempt as a learning opportunity, refining
strategies based on feedback and outcomes.
```

Exercise: Marketing Innovation Workshop

Personalization Experiment:

1. Choose a specific segment of your customer base to target with a personalized marketing campaign.
2. Develop and implement a small-scale campaign tailored to the preferences and behaviors of this segment.
3. Monitor and analyze engagement metrics, feedback, and conversion rates to assess the effectiveness of your personalization strategies.
4. Use insights gathered to iterate and refine your approach for future campaigns.

Experiential Marketing Plan:

1. Brainstorm ideas for an experiential marketing event or activation that aligns with your brand's values and resonates with your target audience.
2. Outline the concept, including the theme, venue, activities, and interactive elements that will create memorable experiences for participants.
3. Develop an execution plan detailing the logistics, timeline,

budget, and resources required to bring your concept to life.

4. Define key performance indicators (KPIs) and metrics for measuring the success of the event, such as attendance, social media engagement, brand sentiment, and post-event sales.

Social Listening Project:

1. Utilize social media listening tools to monitor conversations, mentions, and sentiment related to your brand across various social media platforms.

2. Gather insights about your brand's perception, audience preferences, and emerging trends or topics of interest.

3. Engage with your audience by responding to comments, addressing concerns, and participating in relevant conversations in a timely and authentic manner.

4. Measure the impact of your social listening efforts on key metrics such as customer sentiment, brand awareness, engagement rates, and customer satisfaction scores. Adjust your strategies based on the insights gained to enhance your brand's online presence and reputation.

Challenge for You:

Identify an aspect of your customer experience that could benefit from innovation. Whether it's through personalization, technology integration, or service enhancement, develop a plan to innovate in this area. Execute a pilot project and measure the results, using customer feedback to iterate and improve.

Conclusion:

Innovation in marketing and customer experience is not just about leveraging new technologies but about reimagining how businesses connect with their customers. This chapter provided insights into adopting innovative strategies and practices that foster deep, meaningful interactions with customers. Through case studies like Spotify and Zappos, we've seen the transformative power of innovation in building brand loyalty and driving business success. As businesses navigate the complexities of the modern market, integrating innovation into marketing and customer experience strategies will be crucial for creating lasting relationships and achieving sustainable growth.

14

Innovation in Operations and Supply Chain: Streamlining for Success

*"Efficiency is doing better what
is already being done."*
— Peter Drucker

I n the intricate dance of modern business, the rhythm is set by the efficiency and agility of operations and supply chain management. This chapter embarks on a journey through the transformative power of innovation within these critical business functions. From the factory floor to the final delivery, innovation is the catalyst that refines processes, enhances productivity, and carves out competitive advantages. We will dissect the elements of operational innovation and supply chain optimization, illuminated by real-life success stories, providing a roadmap for businesses aspiring to redefine efficiency and deliver unparalleled value to their customers.

Opening Anecdote: Delivering the Impossible: FedEx's Overnight Revolution

The story of FedEx's inception is a testament to the revolutionary impact of operational innovation. Founded on the radical idea of overnight delivery, FedEx transformed the logistics industry with its hub-and-spoke model, ensuring fast and reliable package delivery. This innovation not only created a new market but also set new standards for speed and efficiency in logistics.

> **Quick Thought:**
> *Innovation in operations and supply chain is about envisioning the art of the possible — turning everyday tasks into opportunities for efficiency, sustainability, and competitive advantage.*

Entrepreneurship in Action: Key Ingredients

- **Technology Integration:** Leveraging cutting-edge technologies such as AI, IoT, and blockchain to enhance visibility, improve accuracy, and automate routine tasks.
- **Process Optimization:** Adopting lean manufacturing principles and continuous improvement methodologies to eliminate waste and streamline processes.
- **Sustainable Practices:** Implementing green supply chain initiatives and sustainable operations to not only reduce environmental impact but also meet the growing consumer demand for responsible business practices.

Case Study: Tesla's Revolution in Manufacturing

Tesla Motors, at its inception, sought not just to introduce electric vehicles (EVs) to the market but to fundamentally transform the automotive industry's approach to manufacturing. Armed with a vision of highly automated and innovative production lines, Tesla aimed to overcome the myriad challenges associated with manufacturing EVs at scale. This included pioneering advancements in battery technology, improving assembly efficiency, and reimagining supply chain logistics to support its ambitious goals.

The Vision: Tesla set out to redefine the automotive industry through electric vehicles produced in highly automated and innovative factories.

The Challenge: Manufacturing electric vehicles at scale required overcoming significant challenges in battery production, assembly efficiency, and supply chain management.

The Strategy: Tesla invested heavily in automation, custom-built machinery, and innovative assembly techniques, such as the Gigafactory for battery production and the use of aluminum welding in car assembly.

The Impact: These innovations have allowed Tesla to scale up production rapidly, reduce costs, and maintain control over the quality and supply chain of critical components, solidifying its leadership in the electric vehicle market.

Case Study: IKEA's Sustainable Supply Chain

IKEA, the world-renowned furniture retailer, set its sights on leading the retail industry towards a more sustainable future. The company's vision was centered on responsible sourcing and environmental stewardship, recognizing the substantial challenge of implementing sustainable practices across its vast, global supply chain. IKEA committed to transforming its supply chain operations by introducing stringent environmental and social standards for suppliers and investing in initiatives that would significantly reduce its ecological footprint, all while demonstrating that sustainability can be an integral part of successful global business operations.

The Vision: IKEA aimed to become a leader in sustainability within the retail sector, focusing on responsible sourcing and environmental stewardship.

The Challenge: Implementing sustainable practices across a global supply chain involving thousands of suppliers and products.

The Strategy: IKEA introduced the IWAY standard, setting strict requirements for suppliers on environmental performance and social responsibility, and invested in renewable energy projects to power its operations.

The Impact: These initiatives have significantly reduced IKEA's environmental footprint, enhanced its brand reputation, and demonstrated that sustainability can be integrated successfully into global supply chains.

Pro Tip: Embrace change as a constant. The world of operations and supply chain is ever-evolving; staying ahead requires a willingness to continuously explore new innovations, adapt processes, and rethink traditional models.

Exercise: Operational Excellence Workshop

Technology Audit:

1. Evaluate your current operations and supply chain to identify areas where technology could enhance efficiency, productivity, or decision-making processes.
2. Select at least one specific process or task that could benefit from automation, digitalization, or the implementation of new technologies.
3. Research and explore technological solutions or tools that align with your identified needs and objectives.
4. Develop a plan for integrating the chosen technology into your operations, considering factors such as implementation costs, training requirements, and potential benefits.

Lean Assessment:

1. Choose a specific operational area or process within your organization to assess using lean principles.
2. Conduct a thorough analysis of the selected process to identify any sources of waste, inefficiencies, or bottlenecks.
3. Apply lean methodologies, such as value stream mapping or 5S principles, to streamline the process and eliminate non-value-added activities.
4. Develop an action plan outlining the steps required to implement lean improvements, assign responsibilities, and establish key performance indicators (KPIs) to measure progress and success.

Sustainability Challenge:

1. Select one aspect of your organization's supply chain, such as sourcing, transportation, packaging, or waste management, to focus on improving sustainability.
2. Conduct a comprehensive assessment of the chosen aspect to identify current environmental impacts, risks, and opportunities for improvement.
3. Develop a sustainability plan that outlines specific goals, targets, and initiatives for reducing environmental footprint and promoting sustainable practices.
4. Implement your sustainability plan, monitor progress, and regularly review and update strategies to ensure continuous improvement and alignment with sustainability objectives.

Challenge for You:

Select an operational process within your organization that has remained unchanged for years. Apply innovative thinking to redesign this process, incorporating technology, lean principles, or sustainability considerations. Implement a pilot project to test the new approach and measure the outcomes.

Conclusion:

Innovation in operations and supply chain is not merely an option but a necessity for businesses aiming to thrive in the contemporary marketplace. Through strategic integration of technology, commitment to process optimization, and dedication to sustainable practices, companies can unlock unprecedented efficiencies and competitive advantages. This chapter has illuminated the path toward operational excellence, showcasing how embracing innovation can transform the backbone of your business. As we continue to navigate the complexities of the business world, let the principles of operational and supply chain innovation guide your journey toward creating lasting value and achieving enduring success.

15

Scaling Innovation: Magnifying Impact

"Greatness is sifted through the grind, therefore don't despise the hard work now for surely it will be worth it in the end."
— Sanjo Jendayi

S caling innovation is not just about amplifying a single idea; it's about embedding a process that perpetually rejuvenates and expands the organizational fabric. This concluding chapter embarks on deciphering the intricate tapestry of scaling innovation, bridging the chasm between ideation and widespread impact. Through strategic insights, real-life exemplars, and a pragmatic approach, we unfold the blueprint for entrepreneurs eager to escalate their innovations from localized successes to global phenomena, ensuring their ventures not only flourish but dominate in an ever-evolving marketplace.

Opening Anecdote: The Growth Engine: Dropbox's Referral Mastery

Dropbox's journey from a simple idea to solve a personal frustration to becoming a cloud storage behemoth embodies the essence of scaling innovation. Initially designed to ease file sharing and storage, Dropbox's founders faced the challenge of scaling their user base. Through a simple yet ingenious referral program, they exponentially increased their user base, showcasing the power of creative strategies in scaling innovation.

> **Quick Thought:**
> *Scaling innovation is akin to nurturing a tree; it requires patience, the right environment, and continuous care to grow from a sapling into a towering giant.*

Entrepreneurship in Action: Key Ingredients

- **Adaptability and Flexibility:** Remaining agile, allowing the innovation process to evolve with market and internal feedback.
- **Strategic Partnerships:** Forming alliances that complement and enhance the innovation's reach and capabilities.
- **Customer-Centric Continuation:** Keeping the consumer at the heart of innovation, ensuring scalability does not compromise value.

Case Study: Shopify's E-commerce Revolution

Shopify embarked on an ambitious mission to revolutionize the e-commerce landscape, aiming to make the dream of running an online store a reality for everyone, from budding entrepreneurs to established businesses. At a time when creating an online presence required significant technical skills and resources, Shopify envisioned a platform that would break down these barriers, offering user-friendly solutions that empower users to launch, manage, and scale their online stores with unparalleled ease. This initiative sought not just to change how individuals and businesses approached e-commerce, but to fundamentally democratize it, opening up new opportunities for retail innovation and entrepreneurship on a global scale.

The Vision: Shopify aimed to democratize e-commerce, making online store creation accessible to everyone, regardless of technical expertise.

The Challenge: Expanding beyond a niche market to become a global platform without losing simplicity and user-friendliness.

The Strategy: Continuous platform enhancements, strategic partnerships, and community building, alongside maintaining a focus on user experience.

The Impact: Shopify now powers millions of businesses worldwide, revolutionizing how retailers operate online, and significantly impacting the global e-commerce landscape.

Case Study: Slack's Growth Through Integration

In the realm of workplace communication, Slack emerged with a bold vision: to streamline and enhance the way teams interact, collaborate, and get work done. Amid a landscape filled with traditional and entrenched communication tools, Slack aimed to set itself apart by creating a platform that was not only more efficient but also highly integrated with a multitude of work-related applications. By prioritizing seamless integration, user experience, and community engagement, Slack positioned itself as a central hub for workplace communication, challenging conventional practices and transforming the dynamics of team collaboration in the digital era.

The Vision: Slack sought to transform workplace communication, making it more efficient and integrated.

The Challenge: Scaling in a market crowded with established communication tools while maintaining a unique value proposition.

The Strategy: Focusing on seamless integrations with other work tools, enhancing user experience, and fostering a strong community of developers.

The Impact: Slack has become a pivotal tool in modern workplaces, exemplifying how focusing on user needs and integration can scale innovation.

```
Pro Tip: Cultivate resilience and a growth mindset.
The journey of scaling innovation is fraught with
challenges and setbacks; resilience ensures you stay
the course, and a growth mindset encourages
continuous learning and adaptation.
```

Exercise: Scaling Innovation Workshop

Assessment of Scalability:

1. Evaluate your current innovation or business model to assess its scalability potential. Consider factors such as growth projections, resource requirements, and operational capabilities.
2. Identify potential bottlenecks or constraints that could hinder scalability, such as limited production capacity, inefficient processes, or dependencies on key resources.
3. Brainstorm potential solutions or optimizations to address identified bottlenecks and improve scalability. Prioritize initiatives based on their potential impact and feasibility.
4. Develop an action plan outlining the steps required to implement scalability improvements, assign responsibilities, and establish timelines for execution.

Market Expansion Plan:

1. Choose a new market segment or geographic area where you envision expanding your innovation or business.
2. Conduct market research to understand the target audience, competitive landscape, regulatory requirements, and cultural nuances of the new market.
3. Outline a comprehensive expansion plan that includes strategies for market entry, product localization or customization, distribution channels, pricing strategies, and promotional activities.
4. Identify potential partnerships or collaborations that

could facilitate market expansion, such as alliances with local businesses or strategic alliances with industry partners.

Feedback Loop Creation:

1. Develop a systematic approach for collecting and analyzing customer feedback as you scale your innovation or business.
2. Define the channels and methods through which customer feedback will be collected, such as surveys, feedback forms, social media monitoring, or customer interviews.
3. Establish clear processes for analyzing and synthesizing feedback data to extract actionable insights and identify areas for improvement.
4. Implement mechanisms for incorporating customer feedback into decision-making processes, product development cycles, and strategic planning initiatives to drive continuous improvement and innovation.

Challenge for You:

Design a pilot project to test a new scaling strategy for your innovation, whether it's a new market, a partnership, or an operational tweak. Monitor the results closely, ready to iterate and adapt based on the findings.

Conclusion:

As we conclude this exploration of scaling innovation, remember that the journey from a nascent idea to a widespread innovation is both arduous and exhilarating. It demands not just creativity and ingenuity but a steadfast commitment to vision, strategy, and the relentless pursuit of growth. This chapter has aimed to arm you with the insights and frameworks to navigate this journey, highlighted by the transformative stories of Dropbox, Shopify, and Slack. Embrace these principles as you endeavor to scale your innovations, knowing that each step forward magnifies your impact on the world.

Epilogue: Beyond the Horizon: A Vision for Tomorrow

As we draw the curtains on this insightful journey through "Daring Disruption," we stand at the precipice of a new dawn in entrepreneurship. The voyage through these chapters has not just been an exploration of concepts but a clarion call to action for every entrepreneur who dreams of leaving an indelible mark on the fabric of industry and society.

Recap of Key Takeaways and Insights from the Book: From the germination of innovative ideas to the scaling of groundbreaking innovations, we've navigated the multifaceted landscape of entrepreneurship. Each chapter served as a beacon, illuminating the path to mastering the art of innovation, understanding the nuances of intellectual property, and embracing the dynamism of marketing and customer experience. We've witnessed the transformative power of disruptive thinking and the strategic maneuvers necessary to navigate complex market landscapes.

Empowering Ongoing Growth: Yet, our journey does not end here. In fact, it's merely the beginning. As you close this book, remember that the true essence of entrepreneurship lies not just in absorbing knowledge but in applying it with relentless determination. It's about taking the lessons learned and forging ahead, braving the unknown with courage and conviction.

Charting Your Course: As you embark on your entrepreneurial voyage, keep the spirit of innovation alive in everything you do. Embrace failure as a stepping stone to success, for it is through adversity that we often discover our greatest strengths. Surround yourself with a community of mentors, peers, and supporters who uplift and inspire you along the way.

A Call to Action: Let this epilogue serve as a reminder that the world eagerly awaits the fruits of your labor. The ideas you cultivate, the innovations you scale, and the impact you create have the power to reshape industries, uplift communities, and leave an enduring legacy for generations to come.

Conclusion: With boundless opportunities on the horizon, fueled by the fire of your entrepreneurial spirit, go forth and dare to disrupt. Seize the day, embrace the challenges, and unleash the full extent of your potential. For in the realm of entrepreneurship, the journey is as exhilarating as the destination, and the possibilities are as vast as the boundless expanse of the entrepreneurial spirit.

The Ask

Dear Trailblazer,

Thank you for journeying with us through the thrilling landscapes of "Daring Disruption." I hope it's sparked your imagination, strengthened your resolve, and armed you with insights to navigate the vibrant world of entrepreneurship. If our paths crossed meaningfully, I'd be honored if you shared your experience in an Amazon review.

Your thoughts light the way for others, turning solitary sparks into a guiding constellation for fellow adventurers. Whether you've uncovered revelations, found clarity, or see room for growth, your voice enriches our collective journey towards innovation.

Eager for more? Dive deeper at my Amazon author page (https://www.amazon.com/author/patrickhperrine). Let's continue to share, learn, and inspire together, building a future where every dream has the space to soar.

With heartfelt thanks,
Patrick H. Perrine

About the Author

Patrick H. Perrine is a trailblazing author, mentor, and seasoned entrepreneur with a spirit that exemplifies the essence of entrepreneurship. From his humble beginnings as a paperboy in Minnesota to his emergence as a globally recognized industry leader, his journey epitomizes resilience and determination.

Fueled by an insatiable thirst for knowledge, Patrick opted for university over his senior high school year, setting the stage for his relentless pursuit of personal growth. His tenure with Up-Start, an organization championing educational opportunities for first-generation Americans, ignited his lifelong commitment to empowering others, extending beyond business and into his early philanthropic endeavors.

In his twenties, Patrick served as a Founding Board member for The Point Foundation, the largest LGBTQ scholarship foundation today. His dedication to fostering inclusivity and aiding LGBTQ students in higher education continues to positively impact hundreds of lives.

Patrick's entrepreneurial journey took flight with myPartner.com, an online dating service that addressed a critical gap in the market. Recognized as one of the "Best Matchmakers" and "Most Innovative Online Dating Sites" by the iDate Industry, the venture earned a Certificate of Recognition issued by California Legislature Assemblyman Mark Leno. This marked Patrick's first step in a journey filled with identifying unique opportunities and delivering transformative solutions across industries from skincare to dog tech.

Despite the hurdles encountered, Patrick's determination only amplified. His passion for nurturing startups led him to establish Rincon Hill Advisors. During this period, he served as a Steering Committee member for StartOut, a leading nonprofit fostering queer entrepreneurship, and consulted with Fortune 500 companies like Berkshire Hathaway and Intuit.

Adding to his achievements as an entrepreneur, Patrick became an angel investor. His foresight led him to invest in promising startups like MisterB&B, the world's largest gay hotelier, and Roadster, the leading commerce platform for car buying. His dog tech venture, too, gained recognition, leading to his selection as a NGLCC Pitch Finalist and participant in the Seamless IoT Accelerator, earning a $100,000 investment offer as a program graduate.

Most recently, Patrick served as an Entrepreneur in Residence (EiR) with 500 StartUps, an organization committed to uplifting global economies through entrepreneurship. This role solidified his dedication to guiding and uplifting aspiring entrepreneurs.

With multiple books to his credit, including recent works "Fail Fast, Recover Faster", "Ignite Your Dream", and "Fueling the Fire," Patrick continues to share his journey and insights. His writing reflects his unwavering commitment to guiding entrepreneurs through their unique journeys.

Patrick H. Perrine is more than a summary of his accomplishments. He stands as a testament to the power of determination, innovation, and a generous spirit. His contributions have been acknowledged in global press publications such as Forbes, Advocate, and Mirror, but his most profound impact lies in the lives of the entrepreneurs he's guided, inspired, and empowered. As he continues sharing his wisdom in the 10 volume series "Be A Unicorn: The New Entrepreneur's Ultimate Guide to Success," Patrick personifies the quintessential entrepreneurial journey—one of resilience, innovation, and the relentless pursuit of personal growth.

Subscribe to my newsletter:
✉ https://patrickperrine.com

Also by Patrick H. Perrine

Your next adventure in entrepreneurship awaits! Choose your guidebook on Amazon (https://www.amazon.com/author/patrickhperrine) or **www.PatrickPerrine.com**, and ignite the spark that takes your venture to new heights. The future is yours to shape!

Unicorn Rising: Ascending to the Pinnacle of Entrepreneurship and the Billionaire's Club

Fueled by entrepreneurial dreams and the allure of the Unicorn Club? Patrick H. Perrine is your guide, offering an unparalleled roadmap set to be every entrepreneur's playbook.

"Unicorn Rising" emerges as the cornerstone of the *Be A Unicorn* series, laying the groundwork that "Daring Disruption" and the other nine volumes build upon.

This seminal work provides an in-depth exploration into the entrepreneurial journey, offering a comprehensive roadmap for those aiming to scale their ventures to the heights of the Unicorn Club.

Driven by the dream of entrepreneurial excellence and a place in the Unicorn Club? Patrick H. Perrine offers an unmatched guide, positioning this book as the ultimate playbook for entrepreneurs.

Within "Unicorn Rising," readers will find a guide not just to achieving lofty valuations, but to navigating the realms of innovation, transformative leadership, and enduring success. It offers insights into the nuances of leadership, the forefront of emerging technologies, financial mastery, and the core of impactful entrepreneurship.

This series acknowledges the uniqueness of each entrepreneurial journey. Patrick delivers foundational wisdom alongside practical tools, emphasizing the tailored path each startup must navigate. Whether you're just beginning your entrepreneurial quest or are a seasoned professional fine-tuning your strategy, this book, and its series, light the way.

Step forward, challenge the status quo, and with "Unicorn Rising," ascend to unprecedented heights in your entrepreneurial venture.

Ignite Your Dream: The Quintessential Checklist for Aspiring Entrepreneurs
Ignite Your Dream: The Quintessential Checklist for Aspiring Entrepreneurs" by Patrick H. Perrine is an immersive guide lighting the path towards entrepreneurial success.

This power-packed handbook propels you from dreaming to achieving with a carefully curated 100-step map. Dive into real-life entrepreneur stories, extract wisdom, and utilize actionable checklists. This book transcends theoretical guidelines, providing a mentorship experience designed to turn dreams into reality.

Ready to kindle your entrepreneurial spirit? "Ignite your Dream" is your step forward towards unlocking potential and achieving success in the exciting world of entrepreneurship.

Fail Fast, Recover Faster: Bouncing Back From Entrepreneurial Failure

Embrace failure and bounce back stronger with "Fail Fast, Recover Faster: Bouncing Back From Entrepreneurial Failure". It's your guidebook through the tumultuous journey of entrepreneurship, celebrating stumbles as stepping stones towards success.

Dive into compelling tales of triumphant entrepreneurs, learn how to pivot rapidly, manage fallout, and convert setbacks into launchpads. Discover strategies for repairing financial, relationship, and reputation damage, and see your failures as badges of resilience.

This transformative book readies you to rebound from failure swiftly, turning your setbacks into your next entrepreneurial triumph. With "Fail Fast, Recover Faster", you're poised to harness your own unicorn moment and turn failure into a launching pad for success.

Fueling the Fire: Nurturing Resilience and Preventing Burnout in Entrepreneurship

In "Fueling the Fire: Nurturing Resilience and Preventing Burnout in Entrepreneurship," seasoned entrepreneur Patrick H. Perrine guides you through the entrepreneurial journey, sharing practical strategies for maintaining resilience and passion.

Drawing from 20 years of startup experience, Perrine covers everything from ideation to acquisition. Discover how to build a support system, manage your time effectively, cultivate a positive work culture, and align your work with your values.

Whether you're an experienced entrepreneur or just beginning, "Fueling the Fire" is a must-read for maintaining balance and fulfillment in the dynamic world of entrepreneurship.